AI
Autonomous Cars
Emergence

Practical Advances in
Artificial Intelligence and Machine Learning

Dr. Lance B. Eliot, MBA, PhD

ISBN: 1-7332498-3-4
ISBN-13: 978-1-7332498-3-6

DEDICATION

To my incredible daughter, Lauren, and my incredible son, Michael.

Forest fortuna adiuvat (from the Latin; good fortune favors the brave).

CONTENTS

Lance B. Eliot

ACKNOWLEDGMENTS

I have been the beneficiary of advice and counsel by many friends, colleagues, family, investors, and many others. I want to thank everyone that has aided me throughout my career. I write from the heart and the head, having experienced first-hand what it means to have others around you that support you during the good times and the tough times.

To Warren Bennis, one of my doctoral advisors and ultimately a colleague, I offer my deepest thanks and appreciation, especially for his calm and insightful wisdom and support.

To Mark Stevens and his generous efforts toward funding and supporting the USC Stevens Center for Innovation.

To Lloyd Greif and the USC Lloyd Greif Center for Entrepreneurial Studies for their ongoing encouragement of founders and entrepreneurs.

To Peter Drucker, William Wang, Aaron Levie, Peter Kim, Jon Kraft, Cindy Crawford, Jenny Ming, Steve Milligan, Chis Underwood, Frank Gehry, Buzz Aldrin, Steve Forbes, Bill Thompson, Dave Dillon, Alan Fuerstman, Larry Ellison, Jim Sinegal, John Sperling, Mark Stevenson, Anand Nallathambi, Thomas Barrack, Jr., and many other innovators and leaders that I have met and gained mightily from doing so.

Thanks to Ed Trainor, Kevin Anderson, James Hickey, Wendell Jones, Ken Harris, DuWayne Peterson, Mike Brown, Jim Thornton, Abhi Beniwal, Al Biland, John Nomura, Eliot Weinman, John Desmond, and many others for their unwavering support during my career.

And most of all thanks as always to Lauren and Michael, for their ongoing support and for having seen me writing and heard much of this material during the many months involved in writing it. To their patience and willingness to listen.

Lance B. Eliot

INTRODUCTION

This is a book that provides the newest innovations and the latest Artificial Intelligence (AI) advances about the emerging nature of AI-based autonomous self-driving driverless cars. Via recent advances in Artificial Intelligence (AI) and Machine Learning (ML), we are nearing the day when vehicles can control themselves and will not require and nor rely upon human intervention to perform their driving tasks (or, that <u>allow</u> for human intervention, but only *require* human intervention in very limited ways).

Similar to my other related books, which I describe in a moment and list the chapters in the Appendix A of this book, I am particularly focused on those advances that pertain to self-driving cars. The phrase "autonomous vehicles" is often used to refer to any kind of vehicle, whether it is ground-based or in the air or sea, and whether it is a cargo hauling trailer truck or a conventional passenger car. Though the aspects described in this book are certainly applicable to all kinds of autonomous vehicles, I am focused more so here on cars.

Indeed, I am especially known for my role in aiding the advancement of self-driving cars, serving currently as the Executive Director of the Cybernetic AI Self-Driving Cars Institute.. In addition to writing software, designing and developing systems and software for self-driving cars, I also speak and write quite a bit about the topic. This book is a collection of some of my more advanced essays. For those of you that might have seen my essays posted elsewhere, I have updated them and integrated them into this book as one handy cohesive package.

You might be interested in companion books that I have written that provide additional key innovations and fundamentals about self-driving cars. Those books are entitled **"Introduction to Driverless Self-Driving Cars," "Advances in AI and Autonomous Vehicles: Cybernetic Self-Driving Cars," "Self-Driving Cars: "The Mother of All AI Projects," "Innovation and Thought Leadership on Self-Driving Driverless Cars," "New Advances in AI Autonomous Driverless Self-Driving Cars," "Autonomous Vehicle Driverless Self-Driving Cars and Artificial Intelligence," "Transformative Artificial Intelligence**

Driverless Self-Driving Cars," "Disruptive Artificial Intelligence and Driverless Self-Driving Cars, and "State-of-the-Art AI Driverless Self-Driving Cars," and "Top Trends in AI Self-Driving Cars," and "AI Innovations and Self-Driving Cars," "Crucial Advances for AI Driverless Cars," "Sociotechnical Insights and AI Driverless Cars," "Pioneering Advances for AI Driverless Cars" and "Leading Edge Trends for AI Driverless Cars," "The Cutting Edge of AI Autonomous Cars" and "The Next Wave of AI Self-Driving Cars" and "Revolutionary Innovations of AI Self-Driving Cars," and "AI Self-Driving Cars Breakthroughs," "Trailblazing Trends for AI Self-Driving Cars," "Ingenious Strides for AI Driverless Cars," "AI Self-Driving Cars Inventiveness," "Visionary Secrets of AI Driverless Cars," "Spearheading AI Self-Driving Cars," "Spurring AI Self-Driving Cars," "Avant-Garde AI Driverless Cars," "AI Self-Driving Cars Evolvement," "AI Driverless Cars Chrysalis," "Boosting AI Autonomous Cars," "AI Self-Driving Cars Trendsetting," and "AI Autonomous Cars Forefront, "AI Autonomous Cars Emergence" (they are all available via Amazon). Appendix A has a listing of the chapters covered.

For this book, I am going to borrow my introduction from those companion books, since it does a good job of laying out the landscape of self-driving cars and my overall viewpoints on the topic. The remainder of this book is material that does not appear in the companion books.

INTRODUCTION TO SELF-DRIVING CARS

This is a book about self-driving cars. Someday in the future, we'll all have self-driving cars and this book will perhaps seem antiquated, but right now, we are at the forefront of the self-driving car wave. Daily news bombards us with flashes of new announcements by one car maker or another and leaves the impression that within the next few weeks or maybe months that the self-driving car will be here. A casual non-technical reader would assume from these news flashes that in fact we must be on the cusp of a true self-driving car. Here's a real news flash: We are still quite a distance from having a true self-driving car. It is years to go before we get there.

Why is that? Because a true self-driving car is akin to a moonshot. In the same manner that getting us to the moon was an incredible feat, likewise is achieving a true self-driving car. Anybody that suggests or even brashly states that the true self-driving car is nearly here should be viewed with great skepticism. Indeed, you'll see that I often tend to use the word "hogwash" or "crock" when I assess much of the decidedly **fake news** about self-driving cars.

Indeed, I've been writing a popular blog post about self-driving cars and hitting hard on those that try to wave their hands and pretend that we are on the imminent verge of true self-driving cars. For many years, I've been known as the AI Insider. Besides writing about AI, I also develop AI software. I do what I describe. It also gives me insights into what others that are doing AI are really doing versus what it is said they are doing.

Many faithful readers had asked me to pull together my insightful short essays and put them into another book, which you are now holding.

For those of you that have been reading my essays over the years, this collection not only puts them together into one handy package, I also updated the essays and added new material. For those of you that are new to the topic of self-driving cars and AI, I hope you find these essays approachable and informative. I also tend to have a writing style with a bit of a voice, and so you'll see that I am times have a wry sense of humor and poke at conformity.

As a former professor and founder of an AI research lab, I for many years wrote in the formal language of academic writing. I published in referred journals and served as an editor for several AI journals. This writing here is not of the nature, and I have adopted a different and more informal style for these essays. That being said, I also do mention from time-to-time more rigorous material on AI and encourage you all to dig into those deeper and more formal materials if so interested.

I am also an AI practitioner. This means that I write AI software for a living. Currently, I head-up the Cybernetics Self-Driving Car Institute, where we are developing AI software for self-driving cars. I am excited to also report that my son, also a software engineer, heads-up our Cybernetics Self-Driving Car Lab. What I have helped to start, and for which he is an integral part, ultimately he will carry long into the future after I have retired. My daughter, a marketing whiz, also is integral to our efforts as head of our Marketing group. She too will carry forward the legacy now being formulated.

For those of you that are reading this book and have a penchant for writing code, you might consider taking a look at the open source code available for self-driving cars. This is a handy place to start learning how to develop AI for self-driving cars. There are also many new educational courses spring forth. There is a growing body of those wanting to learn about and develop self-driving cars, and a growing body of colleges, labs, and other avenues by which you can learn about self-driving cars.

This book will provide a foundation of aspects that I think will get you ready for those kinds of more advanced training opportunities. If you've already taken those classes, you'll likely find these essays especially interesting as they offer a perspective that I am betting few other instructors or faculty offered to you. These are challenging essays that ask you to think beyond the conventional about self-driving cars.

THE MOTHER OF ALL AI PROJECTS

In June 2017, Apple CEO Tim Cook came out and finally admitted that Apple has been working on a self-driving car. As you'll see in my essays, Apple was enmeshed in secrecy about their self-driving car efforts. We have only been able to read the tea leaves and guess at what Apple has been up to. The notion of an iCar has been floating for quite a while, and self-driving engineers and researchers have been signing tight-lipped Non-Disclosure Agreements (NDA's) to work on projects at Apple that were as shrouded in mystery as any military invasion plans might be.

Tim Cook said something that many others in the Artificial Intelligence (AI) field have been saying, namely, the creation of a self-driving car has got to be the mother of all AI projects. In other words, it is in fact a tremendous moonshot for AI. If a self-driving car can be crafted and the AI works as we hope, it means that we have made incredible strides with AI and that therefore it opens many other worlds of potential breakthrough accomplishments that AI can solve.

Is this hyperbole? Am I just trying to make AI seem like a miracle worker and so provide self-aggrandizing statements for those of us writing the AI software for self-driving cars? No, it is not hyperbole. Developing a true self-driving car is really, really, really hard to do. Let me take a moment to explain why. As a side note, I realize that the Apple CEO is known for at times uttering hyperbole, and he had previously said for example that the year 2012 was "the mother of all years," and he had said that the release of iOS 10 was "the mother of all releases" – all of which does suggest he likes to use the handy "mother of" expression. But, I assure you, in terms of true self-driving cars, he has hit the nail on the head. For sure.

When you think about a moonshot and how we got to the moon, there are some identifiable characteristics and those same aspects can be applied to creating a true self-driving car. You'll notice that I keep putting the word "true" in front of the self-driving car expression. I do so because as per my essay about the various levels of self-driving cars, there are some self-driving cars that are only somewhat of a self-driving car. The somewhat versions are ones that require a human driver to be ready to intervene. In my view, that's not a true self-driving car. A true self-driving car is one that requires no human driver intervention at all. It is a car that can entirely undertake via automation the driving task without any human driver needed. This is the essence of what is known as a Level 5 self-driving car. We are currently at the Level 2 and Level 3 mark, and not yet at Level 5.

Getting to the moon involved aspects such as having big stretch goals, incremental progress, experimentation, innovation, and so on. Let's review how this applied to the moonshot of the bygone era, and how it applies to the self-driving car moonshot of today.

Big Stretch Goal

Trying to take a human and deliver the human to the moon, and bring them back, safely, was an extremely large stretch goal at the time. No one knew whether it could be done. The technology wasn't available yet. The cost was huge. The determination would need to be fierce. Etc. To reach a Level 5 self-driving car is going to be the same. It is a big stretch goal. We can readily get to the Level 3, and we are able to see the Level 4 just up ahead, but a Level 5 is still an unknown as to if it is doable. It should eventually be doable and in the same way that we thought we'd eventually get to the moon, but when it will occur is a different story.

Incremental Progress

Getting to the moon did not happen overnight in one fell swoop. It took years and years of incremental progress to get there. Likewise for self-driving cars. Google has famously been striving to get to the Level 5, and pretty much been willing to forgo dealing with the intervening levels, but most of the other self-driving car makers are doing the incremental route. Let's get a good Level 2 and a somewhat Level 3 going. Then, let's improve the Level 3 and get a somewhat Level 4 going. Then, let's improve the Level 4 and finally arrive at a Level 5. This seems to be the prevalent way that we are going to achieve the true self-driving car.

Experimentation

You likely know that there were various experiments involved in perfecting the approach and technology to get to the moon. As per making incremental progress, we first tried to see if we could get a rocket to go into space and safety return, then put a monkey in there, then with a human, then we went all the way to the moon but didn't land, and finally we arrived at the mission that actually landed on the moon. Self-driving cars are the same way. We are doing simulations of self-driving cars. We do testing of self-driving cars on private land under controlled situations. We do testing of self-driving cars on public roadways, often having to meet regulatory requirements including for example having an engineer or equivalent in the car to take over the controls if needed. And so on. Experiments big and small are needed to figure out what works and what doesn't.

Innovation

There are already some advances in AI that are allowing us to progress toward self-driving cars. We are going to need even more advances. Innovation in all aspects of technology are going to be required to achieve a true self-driving car. By no means do we already have everything in-hand that we need to get there. Expect new inventions and new approaches, new algorithms, etc.

Setbacks

Most of the pundits are avoiding talking about potential setbacks in the progress toward self-driving cars. Getting to the moon involved many setbacks, some of which you never have heard of and were buried at the time so as to not dampen enthusiasm and funding for getting to the moon. A recurring theme in many of my included essays is that there are going to be setbacks as we try to arrive at a true self-driving car. Take a deep breath and be ready. I just hope the setbacks don't completely stop progress. I am sure that it will cause progress to alter in a manner that we've not yet seen in the self-driving car field. I liken the self-driving car of today to the excitement everyone had for Uber when it first got going. Today, we have a different view of Uber and with each passing day there are more regulations to the ride sharing business and more concerns raised. The darling child only stays a darling until finally that child acts up. It will happen the same with self-driving cars.

SELF-DRIVING CARS CHALLENGES

But what exactly makes things so hard to have a true self-driving car, you might be asking. You have seen cruise control for years and years. You've lately seen cars that can do parallel parking. You've seen YouTube videos of Tesla drivers that put their hands out the window as their car zooms along the highway, and seen to therefore be in a self-driving car. Aren't we just needing to put a few more sensors onto a car and then we'll have in-hand a true self-driving car? Nope.

Consider for a moment the nature of the driving task. We don't just let anyone at any age drive a car. Worldwide, most countries won't license a driver until the age of 18, though many do allow a learner's permit at the age of 15 or 16. Some suggest that a younger age would be physically too small to reach the controls of the car. Though this might be the case, we could easily adjust the controls to allow for younger aged and thus smaller stature. It's not their physical size that matters. It's their cognitive development that matters.

To drive a car, you need to be able to reason about the car, what the car can and cannot do. You need to know how to operate the car. You need to know about how other cars on the road drive. You need to know what is allowed in driving such as speed limits and driving within marked lanes. You need to be able to react to situations and be able to avoid getting into accidents. You need to ascertain when to hit your brakes, when to steer clear of a pedestrian, and how to keep from ramming that motorcyclist that just cut you off.

Many of us had taken courses on driving. We studied about driving and took driver training. We had to take a test and pass it to be able to drive. The point being that though most adults take the driving task for granted, and we often "mindlessly" drive our cars, there is a significant amount of cognitive effort that goes into driving a car. After a while, it becomes second nature. You don't especially think about how you drive, you just do it. But, if you watch a novice driver, say a teenager learning to drive, you suddenly realize that there is a lot more complexity to it than we seem to realize.

Furthermore, driving is a very serious task. I recall when my daughter and son first learned to drive. They are both very conscientious people. They wanted to make sure that whatever they did, they did well, and that they did not harm anyone. Every day, when you get into a car, it is probably around 4,000 pounds of hefty metal and plastics (about two tons), and it is a lethal weapon. Think about it. You drive down the street in an object that weighs two tons and with the engine it can accelerate and ram into anything you want to hit. The damage a car can inflict is very scary. Both my children were surprised that they were being given the right to maneuver this monster of a beast that could cause tremendous harm entirely by merely letting go of the steering wheel for a moment or taking your eyes off the road.

In fact, in the United States alone there are about 30,000 deaths per year by auto accidents, which is around 100 per day. Given that there are about 263 million cars in the United States, I am actually more amazed that the number of fatalities is not a lot higher. During my morning commute, I look at all the thousands of cars on the freeway around me, and I think that if all of them decided to go zombie and drive in a crazy maniac way, there would be many people dead. Somehow, incredibly, each day, most people drive relatively safely. To me, that's a miracle right there. Getting millions and millions of people to be safe and sane when behind the wheel of a two ton mobile object, it's a feat that we as a society should admire with pride.

So, hopefully you are in agreement that the driving task requires a great deal of cognition. You don't' need to be especially smart to drive a car, and we've done quite a bit to make car driving viable for even the average dolt. There isn't an IQ test that you need to take to drive a car. If you can read and write, and pass a test, you pretty much can legally drive a car. There are of course some that drive a car and are not legally permitted to do so, plus there are private areas such as farms where drivers are young, but for public roadways in the United States, you can be generally of average intelligence (or less) and be able to legally drive.

This though makes it seem like the cognitive effort must not be much. If the cognitive effort was truly hard, wouldn't we only have Einstein's that could drive a car? We have made sure to keep the driving task as simple as we can, by making the controls easy and relatively standardized, and by having roads that are relatively standardized, and so on. It is as though Disneyland has put their Autopia into the real-world, by us all as a society agreeing that roads will be a certain way, and we'll all abide by the various rules of driving.

A modest cognitive task by a human is still something that stymies AI. You certainly know that AI has been able to beat chess players and be good at other kinds of games. This type of narrow cognition is not what car driving is about. Car driving is much wider. It requires knowledge about the world, which a chess playing AI system does not need to know. The cognitive aspects of driving are on the one hand seemingly simple, but at the same time require layer upon layer of knowledge about cars, people, roads, rules, and a myriad of other "common sense" aspects. We don't have any AI systems today that have that same kind of breadth and depth of awareness and knowledge.

As revealed in my essays, the self-driving car of today is using trickery to do particular tasks. It is all very narrow in operation. Plus, it currently assumes that a human driver is ready to intervene. It is like a child that we have taught to stack blocks, but we are needed to be right there in case the child stacks them too high and they begin to fall over. AI of today is brittle, it is narrow, and it does not approach the cognitive abilities of humans. This is why the true self-driving car is somewhere out in the future.

Another aspect to the driving task is that it is not solely a mind exercise. You do need to use your senses to drive. You use your eyes a vision sensors to see the road ahead. You vision capability is like a streaming video, which your brain needs to continually analyze as you drive. Where is the road? Is there a pedestrian in the way? Is there another car ahead of you? Your senses are relying a flood of info to your brain. Self-driving cars are trying to do the same, by using cameras, radar, ultrasound, and lasers. This is an attempt at mimicking how humans have senses and sensory apparatus.

Thus, the driving task is mental and physical. You use your senses, you use your arms and legs to manipulate the controls of the car, and you use your brain to assess the sensory info and direct your limbs to act upon the controls of the car. This all happens instantly. If you've ever perhaps gotten something in your eye and only had one eye available to drive with, you suddenly realize how dependent upon vision you are. If you have a broken foot with a cast, you suddenly realize how hard it is to control the brake pedal and the accelerator. If you've taken medication and your brain is maybe sluggish, you suddenly realize how much mental strain is required to drive a car.

An AI system that plays chess only needs to be focused on playing chess. The physical aspects aren't important because usually a human moves the chess pieces or the chessboard is shown on an electronic display. Using AI for a more life-and-death task such as analyzing MRI images of patients, this again does not require physical capabilities and instead is done by examining images of bits.

Driving a car is a true life-and-death task. It is a use of AI that can easily and at any moment produce death. For those colleagues of mine that are developing this AI, as am I, we need to keep in mind the somber aspects of this. We are producing software that will have in its virtual hands the lives of the occupants of the car, and the lives of those in other nearby cars, and the lives of nearby pedestrians, etc. Chess is not usually a life-or-death matter.

Driving is all around us. Cars are everywhere. Most of today's AI applications involve only a small number of people. Or, they are behind the scenes and we as humans have other recourse if the AI messes up. AI that is driving a car at 80 miles per hour on a highway had better not mess up. The consequences are grave. Multiply this by the number of cars, if we could put magically self-driving into every car in the USA, we'd have AI running in the 263 million cars. That's a lot of AI spread around. This is AI on a massive scale that we are not doing today and that offers both promise and potential peril.

There are some that want AI for self-driving cars because they envision a world without any car accidents. They envision a world in which there is no car congestion and all cars cooperate with each other. These are wonderful utopian visions.

They are also very misleading. The adoption of self-driving cars is going to be incremental and not overnight. We cannot economically just junk all existing cars. Nor are we going to be able to affordably retrofit existing cars. It is more likely that self-driving cars will be built into new cars and that over many years of gradual replacement of existing cars that we'll see the mix of self-driving cars become substantial in the real-world.

In these essays, I have tried to offer technological insights without being overly technical in my description, and also blended the business, societal, and economic aspects too. Technologists need to consider the non-technological impacts of what they do. Non-technologists should be aware of what is being developed.

We all need to work together to collectively be prepared for the enormous disruption and transformative aspects of true self-driving cars. We all need to be involved in this mother of all AI projects.

WHAT THIS BOOK PROVIDES

What does this book provide to you? It introduces many of the key elements about self-driving cars and does so with an AI based perspective. I weave together technical and non-technical aspects, readily going from being concerned about the cognitive capabilities of the driving task and how the technology is embodying this into self-driving cars, and in the next breath I discuss the societal and economic aspects.

They are all intertwined because that's the way reality is. You cannot separate out the technology per se, and instead must consider it within the milieu of what is being invented and innovated, and do so with a mindset towards the contemporary mores and culture that shape what we are doing and what we hope to do.

WHY THIS BOOK

I wrote this book to try and bring to the public view many aspects about self-driving cars that nobody seems to be discussing.

For business leaders that are either involved in making self-driving cars or that are going to leverage self-driving cars, I hope that this book will enlighten you as to the risks involved and ways in which you should be strategizing about how to deal with those risks.

For entrepreneurs, startups and other businesses that want to enter into the self-driving car market that is emerging, I hope this book sparks your interest in doing so, and provides some sense of what might be prudent to pursue.

For researchers that study self-driving cars, I hope this book spurs your interest in the risks and safety issues of self-driving cars, and also nudges you toward conducting research on those aspects.

For students in computer science or related disciplines, I hope this book will provide you with interesting and new ideas and material, for which you might conduct research or provide some career direction insights for you.

For AI companies and high-tech companies pursuing self-driving cars, this book will hopefully broaden your view beyond just the mere coding and development needed to make self-driving cars.

For all readers, I hope that you will find the material in this book to be stimulating. Some of it will be repetitive of things you already know. But I am pretty sure that you'll also find various eureka moments whereby you'll discover a new technique or approach that you had not earlier thought of. I am also betting that there will be material that forces you to rethink some of your current practices.

I am not saying you will suddenly have an epiphany and change what you are doing. I do think though that you will reconsider or perhaps revisit what you are doing.

For anyone choosing to use this book for teaching purposes, please take a look at my suggestions for doing so, as described in the Appendix. I have found the material handy in courses that I have taught, and likewise other faculty have told me that they have found the material handy, in some cases as extended readings and in other instances as a core part of their course (depending on the nature of the class).

In my writing for this book, I have tried carefully to blend both the practitioner and the academic styles of writing. It is not as dense as is typical academic journal writing, but at the same time offers depth by going into the nuances and trade-offs of various practices.

The word "deep" is in vogue today, meaning getting deeply into a subject or topic, and so is the word "unpack" which means to tease out the underlying aspects of a subject or topic. I have sought to offer material that addresses an issue or topic by going relatively deeply into it and make sure that it is well unpacked.

In any book about AI, it is difficult to use our everyday words without having some of them be misinterpreted. Specifically, it is easy to anthropomorphize AI. When I say that an AI system "knows" something, I do not want you to construe that the AI system has sentience and "knows" in the same way that humans do. They aren't that way, as yet. I have tried to use quotes around such words from time-to-time to emphasize that the words I am using should not be misinterpreted to ascribe true human intelligence to the AI systems that we know of today. If I used quotes around all such words, the book would be very difficult to read, and so I am doing so judiciously. Please keep that in mind as you read the material, thanks.

Some of the material is time-based in terms of covering underway activities, and though some of it might decay, nonetheless I believe you'll find the material useful and informative.

COMPANION BOOKS

1. **"Introduction to Driverless Self-Driving Cars"** by Dr. Lance Eliot
2. **"Innovation and Thought Leadership on Self-Driving Driverless Cars"** by Dr. Lance Eliot
3. **"Advances in AI and Autonomous Vehicles: Cybernetic Self-Driving Cars"** by Dr. Lance Eliot
4. **"Self-Driving Cars: The Mother of All AI Projects"** by Dr. Lance Eliot
5. **"New Advances in AI Autonomous Driverless Self-Driving Cars"** by Dr. Lance Eliot
6. **"Autonomous Vehicle Driverless Self-Driving Cars and Artificial Intelligence"** by Dr. Lance Eliot and Michael B. Eliot
7. **"Transformative Artificial Intelligence Driverless Self-Driving Cars"** by Dr. Lance Eliot
8. **"Disruptive Artificial Intelligence and Driverless Self-Driving Cars"** by Dr. Lance Eliot
9. "State-of-the-Art AI Driverless Self-Driving Cars" by Dr. Lance Eliot
10. **"Top Trends in AI Self-Driving Cars"** by Dr. Lance Eliot
11. **"AI Innovations and Self-Driving Cars"** by Dr. Lance Eliot
12. **"Crucial Advances for AI Driverless Cars"** by Dr. Lance Eliot
13. **"Sociotechnical Insights and AI Driverless Cars"** by Dr. Lance Eliot.
14. **"Pioneering Advances for AI Driverless Cars"** by Dr. Lance Eliot
15. **"Leading Edge Trends for AI Driverless Cars"** by Dr. Lance Eliot
16. **"The Cutting Edge of AI Autonomous Cars"** by Dr. Lance Eliot
17. **"The Next Wave of AI Self-Driving Cars"** by Dr. Lance Eliot
18. **"Revolutionary Innovations of AI Driverless Cars"** by Dr. Lance Eliot
19. **"AI Self-Driving Cars Breakthroughs"** by Dr. Lance Eliot
20. **"Trailblazing Trends for AI Self-Driving Cars"** by Dr. Lance Eliot
21. **"Ingenious Strides for AI Driverless Cars"** by Dr. Lance Eliot
22. **"AI Self-Driving Cars Inventiveness"** by Dr. Lance Eliot
23. **"Visionary Secrets of AI Driverless Cars"** by Dr. Lance Eliot
24. **"Spearheading AI Self-Driving Cars"** by Dr. Lance Eliot
25. **"Spurring AI Self-Driving Cars"** by Dr. Lance Eliot
26. **"Avant-Garde AI Driverless Cars"** by Dr. Lance Eliot
27. **"AI Self-Driving Cars Evolvement"** by Dr. Lance Eliot
28. **"AI Driverless Cars Chrysalis"** by Dr. Lance Eliot
29. **"Boosting AI Autonomous Cars"** by Dr. Lance Eliot
30. **"AI Self-Driving Cars Trendsetting"** by Dr. Lance Eliot
31. **"AI Autonomous Cars Forefront"** by Dr. Lance Eliot
32. **"AI Autonomous Cars Emergence"** by Dr. Lance Eliot

These books are available on Amazon and at other major global booksellers.

CHAPTER 1

ELIOT FRAMEWORK FOR AI SELF-DRIVING CARS

CHAPTER 1

ELIOT FRAMEWORK FOR AI SELF-DRIVING CARS

This chapter is a core foundational aspect for understanding AI self-driving cars and I have used this same chapter in several of my other books to introduce the reader to essential elements of this field. Once you've read this chapter, you'll be prepared to read the rest of the material since the foundational essence of the components of autonomous AI driverless self-driving cars will have been established for you.

When I give presentations about self-driving cars and teach classes on the topic, I have found it helpful to provide a framework around which the various key elements of self-driving cars can be understood and organized (see diagram at the end of this chapter). The framework needs to be simple enough to convey the overarching elements, but at the same time not so simple that it belies the true complexity of self-driving cars. As such, I am going to describe the framework here and try to offer in a thousand words (or more!) what the framework diagram itself intends to portray.

The core elements on the diagram are numbered for ease of reference. The numbering does not suggest any kind of prioritization of the elements. Each element is crucial. Each element has a purpose, and otherwise would not be included in the framework. For some self-driving cars, a particular element might be more important or somehow distinguished in comparison to other self-driving cars.

You could even use the framework to rate a particular self-driving car, doing so by gauging how well it performs in each of the elements of the framework. I will describe each of the elements, one at a time. After doing so, I'll discuss aspects that illustrate how the elements interact and perform during the overall effort of a self-driving car.

At the Cybernetic Self-Driving Car Institute, we use the framework to keep track of what we are working on, and how we are developing software that fills in what is needed to achieve Level 5 self-driving cars.

D-01: Sensor Capture

Let's start with the one element that often gets the most attention in the press about self-driving cars, namely, the sensory devices for a self-driving car.

On the framework, the box labeled as D-01 indicates "Sensor Capture" and refers to the processes of the self-driving car that involve collecting data from the myriad of sensors that are used for a self-driving car. The types of devices typically involved are listed, such as the use of mono cameras, stereo cameras, LIDAR devices, radar systems, ultrasonic devices, GPS, IMU, and so on.

These devices are tasked with obtaining data about the status of the self-driving car and the world around it. Some of the devices are continually providing updates, while others of the devices await an indication by the self-driving car that the device is supposed to collect data. The data might be first transformed in some fashion by the device itself, or it might instead be fed directly into the sensor capture as raw data. At that point, it might be up to the sensor capture processes to do transformations on the data. This all varies depending upon the nature of the devices being used and how the devices were designed and developed.

D-02: Sensor Fusion

Imagine that your eyeballs receive visual images, your nose receives odors, your ears receive sounds, and in essence each of your distinct sensory devices is getting some form of input. The input befits the nature of the device. Likewise, for a self-driving car, the cameras provide visual images, the radar returns radar reflections, and so on.

Each device provides the data as befits what the device does.

At some point, using the analogy to humans, you need to merge together what your eyes see, what your nose smells, what your ears hear, and piece it all together into a larger sense of what the world is all about and what is happening around you. Sensor fusion is the action of taking the singular aspects from each of the devices and putting them together into a larger puzzle.

Sensor fusion is a tough task. There are some devices that might not be working at the time of the sensor capture. Or, there might some devices that are unable to report well what they have detected. Again, using a human analogy, suppose you are in a dark room and so your eyes cannot see much. At that point, you might need to rely more so on your ears and what you hear. The same is true for a self-driving car. If the cameras are obscured due to snow and sleet, it might be that the radar can provide a greater indication of what the external conditions consist of.

In the case of a self-driving car, there can be a plethora of such sensory devices. Each is reporting what it can. Each might have its difficulties. Each might have its limitations, such as how far ahead it can detect an object. All of these limitations need to be considered during the sensor fusion task.

D-03: Virtual World Model

For humans, we presumably keep in our minds a model of the world around us when we are driving a car. In your mind, you know that the car is going at say 60 miles per hour and that you are on a freeway. You have a model in your mind that your car is surrounded by other cars, and that there are lanes to the freeway. Your model is not only based on what you can see, hear, etc., but also what you know about the nature of the world. You know that at any moment that car ahead of you can smash on its brakes, or the car behind you can ram into your car, or that the truck in the next lane might swerve into your lane.

The AI of the self-driving car needs to have a virtual world model, which it then keeps updated with whatever it is receiving from the sensor fusion, which received its input from the sensor capture and the sensory devices.

D-04: System Action Plan

By having a virtual world model, the AI of the self-driving car is able to keep track of where the car is and what is happening around the car. In addition, the AI needs to determine what to do next. Should the self-driving car hit its brakes? Should the self-driving car stay in its lane or swerve into the lane to the left? Should the self-driving car accelerate or slow down?

A system action plan needs to be prepared by the AI of the self-driving car. The action plan specifies what actions should be taken. The actions need to pertain to the status of the virtual world model. Plus, the actions need to be realizable.

This realizability means that the AI cannot just assert that the self-driving car should suddenly sprout wings and fly. Instead, the AI must be bound by whatever the self-driving car can actually do, such as coming to a halt in a distance of X feet at a speed of Y miles per hour, rather than perhaps asserting that the self-driving car come to a halt in 0 feet as though it could instantaneously come to a stop while it is in motion.

D-05: Controls Activation

The system action plan is implemented by activating the controls of the car to act according to what the plan stipulates. This might mean that the accelerator control is commanded to increase the speed of the car. Or, the steering control is commanded to turn the steering wheel 30 degrees to the left or right.

One question arises as to whether or not the controls respond as they are commanded to do. In other words, suppose the AI has commanded the accelerator to increase, but for some reason it does not do so. Or, maybe it tries to do so, but the speed of the car does not increase. The controls activation feeds back into the virtual world model, and simultaneously the virtual world model is getting updated from the sensors, the sensor capture, and the sensor fusion. This allows the AI to ascertain what has taken place as a result of the controls being commanded to take some kind of action.

By the way, please keep in mind that though the diagram seems to have a linear progression to it, the reality is that these are all aspects of the self-driving car that are happening in parallel and simultaneously. The sensors are capturing data, meanwhile the sensor fusion is taking place, meanwhile the virtual model is being updated, meanwhile the system action plan is being formulated and reformulated, meanwhile the controls are being activated.

This is the same as a human being that is driving a car. They are eyeballing the road, meanwhile they are fusing in their mind the sights, sounds, etc., meanwhile their mind is updating their model of the world around them, meanwhile they are formulating an action plan of what to do, and meanwhile they are pushing their foot onto the pedals and steering the car. In the normal course of driving a car, you are doing all of these at once. I mention this so that when you look at the diagram, you will think of the boxes as processes that are all happening at the same time, and not as though only one happens and then the next.

They are shown diagrammatically in a simplistic manner to help comprehend what is taking place. You though should also realize that they are working in parallel and simultaneous with each other. This is a tough aspect in that the inter-element communications involve latency and other aspects that must be taken into account. There can be delays in one element updating and then sharing its latest status with other elements.

D-06: Automobile & CAN

Contemporary cars use various automotive electronics and a Controller Area Network (CAN) to serve as the components that underlie the driving aspects of a car. There are Electronic Control Units (ECU's) which control subsystems of the car, such as the engine, the brakes, the doors, the windows, and so on.

The elements D-01, D-02, D-03, D-04, D-05 are layered on top of the D-06, and must be aware of the nature of what the D-06 is able to do and not do.

D-07: In-Car Commands

Humans are going to be occupants in self-driving cars. In a Level 5 self-driving car, there must be some form of communication that takes place between the humans and the self-driving car. For example, I go into a self-driving car and tell it that I want to be driven over to Disneyland, and along the way I want to stop at In-and-Out Burger. The self-driving car now parses what I've said and tries to then establish a means to carry out my wishes.

In-car commands can happen at any time during a driving journey. Though my example was about an in-car command when I first got into my self-driving car, it could be that while the self-driving car is carrying out the journey that I change my mind. Perhaps after getting stuck in traffic, I tell the self-driving car to forget about getting the burgers and just head straight over to the theme park. The self-driving car needs to be alert to in-car commands throughout the journey.

D-08: V2X Communications

We will ultimately have self-driving cars communicating with each other, doing so via V2V (Vehicle-to-Vehicle) communications. We will also have self-driving cars that communicate with the roadways and other aspects of the transportation infrastructure, doing so via V2I (Vehicle-to-Infrastructure).

The variety of ways in which a self-driving car will be communicating with other cars and infrastructure is being called V2X, whereby the letter X means whatever else we identify as something that a car should or would want to communicate with. The V2X communications will be taking place simultaneous with everything else on the diagram, and those other elements will need to incorporate whatever it gleans from those V2X communications.

D-09: Deep Learning

The use of Deep Learning permeates all other aspects of the self-driving car. The AI of the self-driving car will be using deep learning to do a better job at the systems action plan, and at the controls activation, and at the sensor fusion, and so on.

Currently, the use of artificial neural networks is the most prevalent form of deep learning. Based on large swaths of data, the neural networks attempt to "learn" from the data and therefore direct the efforts of the self-driving car accordingly.

D-10: Tactical AI

Tactical AI is the element of dealing with the moment-to-moment driving of the self-driving car. Is the self-driving car staying in its lane of the freeway? Is the car responding appropriately to the controls commands? Are the sensory devices working?

For human drivers, the tactical equivalent can be seen when you watch a novice driver such as a teenager that is first driving. They are focused on the mechanics of the driving task, keeping their eye on the road while also trying to properly control the car.

D-11: Strategic AI

The Strategic AI aspects of a self-driving car are dealing with the larger picture of what the self-driving car is trying to do. If I had asked that the self-driving car take me to Disneyland, there is an overall journey map that needs to be kept and maintained.

There is an interaction between the Strategic AI and the Tactical AI. The Strategic AI is wanting to keep on the mission of the driving, while the Tactical AI is focused on the particulars underway in the driving effort. If the Tactical AI seems to wander away from the overarching mission, the Strategic AI wants to see why and get things back on track. If the Tactical AI realizes that there is something amiss on the self-driving car, it needs to alert the Strategic AI accordingly and have an adjustment to the overarching mission that is underway.

D-12: Self-Aware AI

Very few of the self-driving cars being developed are including a Self-Aware AI element, which we at the Cybernetic Self-Driving Car Institute believe is crucial to Level 5 self-driving cars.

The Self-Aware AI element is intended to watch over itself, in the sense that the AI is making sure that the AI is working as intended. Suppose you had a human driving a car, and they were starting to drive erratically. Hopefully, their own self-awareness would make them realize they themselves are driving poorly, such as perhaps starting to fall asleep after having been driving for hours on end. If you had a passenger in the car, they might be able to alert the driver if the driver is starting to do something amiss. This is exactly what the Self-Aware

AI element tries to do, it becomes the overseer of the AI, and tries to detect when the AI has become faulty or confused, and then find ways to overcome the issue.

D-13: Economic

The economic aspects of a self-driving car are not per se a technology aspect of a self-driving car, but the economics do indeed impact the nature of a self-driving car. For example, the cost of outfitting a self-driving car with every kind of possible sensory device is prohibitive, and so choices need to be made about which devices are used. And, for those sensory devices chosen, whether they would have a full set of features or a more limited set of features.

We are going to have self-driving cars that are at the low-end of a consumer cost point, and others at the high-end of a consumer cost point. You cannot expect that the self-driving car at the low-end is going to be as robust as the one at the high-end. I realize that many of the self-driving car pundits are acting as though all self-driving cars will be the same, but they won't be. Just like anything else, we are going to have self-driving cars that have a range of capabilities. Some will be better than others. Some will be safer than others. This is the way of the real-world, and so we need to be thinking about the economics aspects when considering the nature of self-driving cars.

D-14: Societal

This component encompasses the societal aspects of AI which also impacts the technology of self-driving cars. For example, the famous Trolley Problem involves what choices should a self-driving car make when faced with life-and-death matters. If the self-driving car is about to either hit a child standing in the roadway, or instead ram into a tree at the side of the road and possibly kill the humans in the self-driving car, which choice should be made?

We need to keep in mind the societal aspects will underlie the AI of the self-driving car. Whether we are aware of it explicitly or not, the AI will have embedded into it various societal assumptions.

D-15: Innovation

I included the notion of innovation into the framework because we can anticipate that whatever a self-driving car consists of, it will continue to be innovated over time. The self-driving cars coming out in the next several years will undoubtedly be different and less innovative than the versions that come out in ten years hence, and so on.

Framework Overall

For those of you that want to learn about self-driving cars, you can potentially pick a particular element and become specialized in that aspect. Some engineers are focusing on the sensory devices. Some engineers focus on the controls activation. And so on. There are specialties in each of the elements.

Researchers are likewise specializing in various aspects. For example, there are researchers that are using Deep Learning to see how best it can be used for sensor fusion. There are other researchers that are using Deep Learning to derive good System Action Plans. Some are studying how to develop AI for the Strategic aspects of the driving task, while others are focused on the Tactical aspects.

A well-prepared all-around software developer that is involved in self-driving cars should be familiar with all of the elements, at least to the degree that they know what each element does. This is important since whatever piece of the pie that the software developer works on, they need to be knowledgeable about what the other elements are doing.

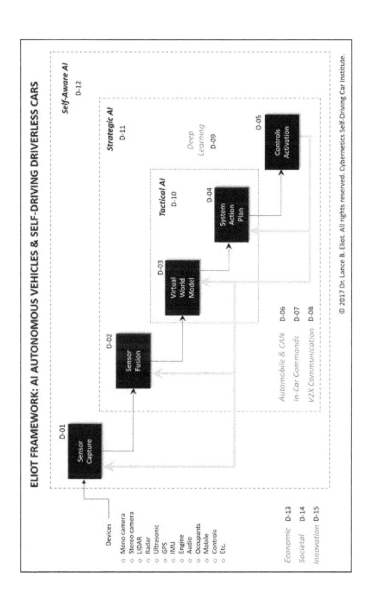

ELIOT FRAMEWORK: AI AUTONOMOUS VEHICLES & SELF-DRIVING DRIVERLESS CARS

CHAPTER 2
DROPPING OFF RIDERS
AND
AI SELF-DRIVING CARS

CHAPTER 2

DROPPING OFF RIDERS
AND AI SELF-DRIVING CARS

I was using a ridesharing service last month in Detroit to get to a restaurant after having spoken at a conference on autonomous vehicles.

The driver decided that trying to stop in front of the restaurant to let me out of the car would be difficult because there were other cars parked there, meaning he'd need to temporarily double-park or at least come to a standstill to let me out, and he'd also be directly in the street, stalling traffic on a rather hectic and tight downtown passageway. He spied instead a bus stop that was wide open, just past the restaurant, though a large group of people were waiting anxiously for a bus to arrive and the marked area or zone clearly said it was exclusively for bus loading and unloading only.

Anyway, undeterred, the driver opted to pull into the bus zone, coming to a rapid stop, and by an unlucky chance for him (and me), sure enough a large bus tried to come into the zone at just that same moment. The ridesharing driver started to yell at me to hurriedly get out of his car since the bus was now directly behind us and things were dicey. Meanwhile, I was gathering up my briefcase and traveling bags, doing so with seemingly not enough haste for the driver, though let's all acknowledge that it was his choice about where to drop me off and obviously was not the most astute move.

Getting Dropped Off Can Be A Dangerous Proposition

I'm sure you've had similar situations involving a ridesharing service or a cab that ended up dumping you onto a spot or location that wasn't the most desirable for being dropped off.

I remember one time, while in New York City, a cab driver was taking me to my hotel after my having arrived past midnight at the airport, and for reasons I'll never know he opted to drop me about a block away from the hotel, doing so at a darkened corner, marked with graffiti, and looking ominous (perhaps it was easier for him to drop me there so as to continue to his next fare). The downside was that I walked a city block at nighttime, in an area that I later discovered was widely known for being dangerous, including muggings and other unsavory acts.

In one sense, when we are dropped off from a ridesharing service or its equivalent, we often tend to assume that the driver has identified a suitable place to do the drop-off.

Presumably, the drop-off is near to the desired destination, it should be relatively easy to get out of the vehicle at the drop-off spot, it should be safe to get out, and overall it is a vital part of the journey and ought to count as much as the pick-up and the drive itself. In my experience, the drop-off often seems to be a time for the driver to get rid of a passenger and in fact the driver's mindset is often on where their next fare will be, since they've now exhausted the value of the existing passenger and are seeking out more revenue from their next candidate passenger.

Of course, you can even undermine yourself when it comes to doing a drop-off.

The other day, it was reported in the news that a woman got out of her car on the 405 freeway in Los Angeles when her car had stalled, and regrettably, horrifically, another car rammed into her and her stalled vehicle.

A cascading series of car crashes then occurred, closing down much of the freeway in that area and backing up traffic for miles.

In some cases, when driving a car ourselves, we make judgements about when to get out of the vehicle, and in other cases such as ridesharing or taking a taxi, we are having someone else make a judgement for us.

In the case of a ridesharing or taxi driver, I eventually figured out that as the customer I need to double-check the drop-off, along with requesting an alternative spot to be dropped off if the circumstances seem to warrant it. You usually though assume that the local driver you are relying on has a better sense as to what is suitable for a drop-off, but the driver might not be thinking about the conditions you face and instead could be concentrating on other matters entirely.

Here's a question for you, how will self-driving driverless autonomous cars know where to drop-off human passengers?

This is actually a quite vexing problem that though not yet seemingly very high on the priority list of AI developers for autonomous cars, ultimately the drop-off matter will rear its problematic head as something needing to be solved.

Why Dropping Off Is Tough For AI

The simplistic view of how the AI should drop you off consists of the AI system merely stopping at the exact location of where you've requested to go, as though it is merely a mathematically specified latitude and longitude, and then it is up to you to get out of the self-driving car.

This might mean that the autonomous car is double-parked, though if this is an illegal traffic act then it goes against the belief that self-driving cars should not be breaking the law.

I've spoken and written extensively that it is a falsehood to think that autonomous cars will always strictly obey all traffic laws, since there are many situations in which we as humans bend or at times violate the strict letter of the traffic laws, doing so because of the necessity of the moment or even at times are allowed to do so.

In any case, my point is that the AI system in this simplistic perspective is not doing what we would overall hope or expect a human driver to do when identifying a drop-off spot, which as I mentioned earlier should have these kinds of characteristics:

- Close to the desired destination

- Stopping at a spot that allows for getting out of the car

- Ensuring the safety of the disembarking passengers

- Ensuring the safety of the car in its stopped posture

- Not marring the traffic during its stop

- Etc.

Imagine for a moment what the AI would need to do to derive a drop-off spot based on those kinds of salient criteria.

The sensors of the self-driving car, such as the cameras, radar, ultrasonic, LIDAR, and other devices would need to be able to collect data in real-time about the surroundings of the destination, once the self-driving car has gotten near to that point, and then the AI needs to figure out where to bring the car to a halt and allow for the disembarking of the passengers. The AI needs to assess what is close to the destination, what might be an unsafe spot to stop, what is the status of traffic that's behind the driverless car, and so on.

Let's also toss other variables into the mix. Suppose it is nighttime, does the drop-off selection change versus when dropping off in daylight (often, the answer is yes). Is it raining or snowing, and if so, does that impact the drop-off choice (usually, yes)? Is there any road repair taking place near to the destination and does that impact the options for doing the drop-off (yes)?

If you are saying to yourself that the passenger ought to take fate into their own hands and tell the AI system where to drop them off, yes, some AI developers are incorporating Natural Language Processing (NLP) that can interact with the passengers for such situations, though this does not entirely solve this drop-off problem.

Why?

Because the passenger might not know what is a good place to drop-off. I've had situations whereby I argued with a ridesharing driver or cabbie about where I thought I should be dropped-off, yet it turned out their local knowledge was more attune to what was a prudent and safer place to do so.

Plus, in the case of autonomous cars, keep in mind that the passengers in the driverless car might be all children and no adults. This means that you are potentially going to have a child trying to decide what is the right place to be dropped off.

I shudder to think if we are really going to have an AI system that lacks any semblance of common-sense be taking strict orders from a young child, whereas an adult human driver would be able to counteract any naïve and dangerous choice of drop-offs (presumably, hopefully).

Conclusion

The drop-off topic will especially come to play for self-driving cars at a Level 4, which is the level at which an autonomous car will seek to pullover or find a "minimal risk condition" setting when the AI has reached a point that it has exhausted its allowed Operational Design Domain (ODD). We are going to have passengers inside Level 4 self-driving cars that might get stranded in places that are not prudent for them, including say young children or perhaps someone elderly and having difficulty caring for their own well-being.

It has been reported that some of the initial tryouts of self-driving cars revealed that the autonomous cars got flummoxed somewhat when approaching a drop-off at a busy schoolground, which makes sense in that even as a human driver the chaotic situation of young kids running in and around cars at a school can be unnerving. I remember when my children were youngsters how challenging it was to wade into the morass of cars coming and going at the start of school day and at the end of the school day.

One solution apparently for the reported case of the self-driving cars involved re-programming the drop- off of its elementary school aged passengers at a corner down the street from the school, thus apparently staying out of the traffic foray. In the case of my own children, I had considered doing something similar, but subsequently realized that it meant they had a longer distance to walk to school, providing other potential untoward aspects and that it made more sense to dig into the traffic and drop them as closely to the school entrance as I could get.

Some hope that Machine Learning and Deep Learning will gradually improve the AI driving systems as to where to drop=off people, potentially learning over time where to do so, though I caution that this is not a slam-dunk notion (partially due to the lack of common-sense reasoning for AI today).

Others say that we'll just all have to adjust to the primitive AI systems and have all restaurants, stores, and other locales all stipulate a designated drop-off zone. This seems like an arduous logistics aspect that would be unlikely for all possible drop-off situations. Another akin approach involves using V2V (vehicle-to-vehicle) electronic communications, allowing a car that has found a drop-off spot to inform other nearing cars as to where the drop-off is. Once again, this has various trade-offs and is not a cure-all.

It might seem like a ridiculous topic to some, the idea of worrying about dropping off people from autonomous cars just smacks of being an overkill kind of matter. Just get to the desired destination via whatever coordinates are available, and make sure the autonomous car doesn't hit anything or anyone while getting there.

The thing is, the last step, getting out of an autonomous car, might ruin your day, or worse lose a life, and we need to consider holistically the entire passenger journey from start to finish, including where to drop-off the humans riding in self-driving driverless cars.

It will be one small step for mankind, and one giant leap for autonomous cars.

CHAPTER 3
ADD-ON KITS DRIVE.AI
AND
AI SELF-DRIVING CARS

CHAPTER 3

ADD-ON KITS DRIVE.AI
AND
AI SELF-DRIVING CARS

A relatively smallish company named Drive.AI that had embarked upon trying to develop self-driving car tech has closed its doors and otherwise been acquired by Apple.

Presumably, the AI developers are being acqui-hired, a form of hiring of tech talent via acquisition of the firm that they were in, and in this case will consist of developers being melded into Apple's myriad of AI efforts including the secretive Project Titan autonomous car project.

Various speculation has been made about what led to the demise of Drive.AI.

The firm was started in 2015 by an outcropping of Stanford's AI Lab and over time gradually raised an estimated $77 million to pursue self-driving driverless vehicles, eventually at its peak being valued at perhaps $200 million (per speculation).

They had made some progress in their endeavor and launched several pilot efforts on public roadways, reaching beyond their core efforts in Mountain View, California and San Francisco environs to undertake a rather higher profile operation in Frisco, Texas. The Texas tryouts involved providing a short-haul driverless shuttle-like service to Cowboy's football games, doing so with brightly marked orange vans.

Those of us inside the autonomous car realm knew that the firm was on the ropes and that the execs had been quietly asking around to find a potential buyer. In the end, Apple decided to bite on the apple, as it were, and reportedly ended-up with a modest fleet of Lincoln MKZ's, Audi A4's, and Nissan NV200's, now converted into a variant of driverless capabilities, and were able to pick-and-choose the talent that they wanted to grab, likely also taking ownership of potentially valuable assets such as Intellectual Property (IP) of the defunct firm.

I'd like to offer one key factor that I assert was a nail in the coffin of this particular self-driving driverless car startup, namely their affection for trying to develop an add-on kit that would be able to miraculously convert a car or vehicle into becoming a driverless autonomous one.

Let's unpack my assertion.

Nirvana Goal Of A Universal Add-On Kit For Making Driverless Cars

If you were anointed to be the head of an automaker or tech firm that was trying to develop truly autonomous cars, meaning cars that are driven entirely by AI and there is no need and not even a provision for human driving in the car, how would you approach this moonshot sized task?

I say moonshot because unlike those that seem to think that forging a driverless car is a relatively easy development effort, let's set the record straight and acknowledge it is a Herculean mission. As Tim Cook had earlier stated some years ago, trying to craft a truly autonomous car is the mother of all development projects.

Keep in mind that you aren't especially building a car or vehicle per se, instead you are attempting to build a driver.

You are seeking to create an AI system that embodies many of the same capabilities that a human driver has. I know that some sneer when they hear the phrase of a "human driver" and tend to denigrate how lousy humans are as drivers, but this snarky viewpoint completely belies the actual and amazing cognitive effort that humans deploy to safely drive a car.

Okay, so back to my question, how would you as the CEO of a newly borne driverless car project go about developing a fully autonomous car?

Well, you could aim at whatever brand or models of cars that your firm already made and try to integrate into those cars the various high-tech sensors and other sophisticated tech aspects needed to infuse self-driving capabilities into the vehicle.

That's indeed what most of the automakers and tech firms are doing.

Or, you could try to really swing for the fences and seek to craft a universal add-on kit that would be plopped onto any car or vehicle and allow you to convert the vehicle into being a true driverless version.

The reason this is said to be a swing for the fences is partially due to the outsized potential that such an approach has.

Right now, most would generally agree that the existing 250 million conventional cars in the United States alone will eventually end-up on the junk heap and never become driverless cars. We'll have new driverless cars being gradually produced by the automakers and as those newfangled cars come into the marketplace, there will be people that opt to sell-off their conventional car or send it to the scrap yard, and replace it with the fancier and more exciting (and useful) autonomous cars.

But, wait a second, suppose you could craft an add-on kit that would allow those 250 million cars to be repurposed into becoming driverless cars. Whoa! That's a brilliant idea, some say.

Rather than scrapping those cars, convert them into modernized self-driving cars.

And, the money making is outrageously obscene, since you can simply multiply the cost of the conversion and the hardware kit by the multiplier of 250 million and you end-up with a big number (plus, there are an estimated 1 billion cars all-told in the world, so you could assume that some portion of those outside the U.S. you could also convert).

Drive.AI had made several pivots during its existence, of which they originally started with the retrofit kit-making approach and kept it ingrained in much of what they did, hoping to do two things at once, get public roadway trials underway with cars they had converted into being driverless, and simultaneously try to keep the driverless capability as its own kind of standalone capability that could be applied over and over again to essentially any kind of car.

It's a reach that some might argue was a bridge to far, perhaps biting off more than can be chewed, given the complexity and enormity of the effort to develop initial driverless cars.

Consider The Add-On Kit Notion

One of the reasons that making a universal add-on kit problematic is due to the variability across different lines of cars, given that each automaker can pretty much design and devise the car controls and other automotive capabilities as they so wish (limited to the extent that they must meet federal guidelines, if deploying in the United States).

The wider you want your kit scope to be, the harder the task of creating such a kit becomes.

The narrower you are willing to shape your scope, such as say a particular car line or a specific brand or a model, the more the chances of achieving a viable kit will tend to rise (though, you are obviously then limiting the expanse of where it can be applied).

The top of the nirvana heap would be a universal add-on kit that achieves a truly autonomous car and that could be installed as a DIY (Do It Yourself) effort on any make or model of car.

This would mean that consumers that had at least some modicum of car mechanics skills could buy the kit and proceed to install it themselves onto their car, whatever type of car they might happen to own.

I'll say right now you ought to forget that notion since it is just too far beyond reality, at least for now.

Also, please note that some earlier start-ups in the driverless car space made a lot of splash about how they were going to make and provide add-on kits, but the truth of the matter was that these kits had little to do with a car becoming a true Level 5 autonomous car, and were instead very simplistic semi-autonomous (at best) add-ons, allowing you to kind of make a car into having Advanced Driver Assistance Systems (ADAS) capabilities, kind of, maybe, sort of.

I tried to warn about these headline grabbing stunts and was relived to see that such offerings eventually fell by the wayside. They were easy to spot because they often involved Rube Goldberg looking contraptions that you would mount on your steering wheel and floor pedals, which made things look as though some crazy robotic appendages had crawled into your car and were seeking to overtake humanity.

Not prudent, not safe, incomplete, and didn't last.

You can aim at a DIFM (Do It For Me) approach, rather than a DIY market, in which you would have specially trained and likely certified car technicians that would install your add-on kit.

This too is currently out-of-reach.

In the end, right now, the feasible approach involves working behind-the-scenes with a particular automaker to craft and shape your driverless car collection of sensors, processors, and other gear to be a tight fit to the particular car and then see how things go from there.

Conclusion

An aspect that many don't see and that's happening under-the-hood, as it were, involves the software that is running the hardware gear that aids in making a car become autonomous.

The software can be written in a very tailored manner, which is the easiest way to code it when you are under-the-gun to get a driverless car system up and going. Same goes for the Machine Learning and Deep Learning aspects.

Unfortunately, the tailorization and embedding of specifics means that the software will be difficult to port over to the next driverless car that you seek to do. It becomes a one trick pony, and you can't say for sure if it will work on the next project you undertake, or that if it will be reworkable then how much of an effort will be needed to reshape it accordingly.

As those of us in the AI development business say, you can't especially embrace style when you are in a street fight.

The pressures are enormous to get to a driverless car first, doing so right now or ASAP, a desire to not only amaze the world, but also because the world is watching and making decisions about which automakers and tech firms are winning in this realm and which are not. Those that are perceived as not getting their wares onto the public roadways are dinged as laggards, even though the truth might be that they could be a lot farther along than some of the splashier news-raking ones.

So, if your recourse as an AI developer of gaining speed-to-market means that you have to do idiosyncratic stuff that won't readily be portable, you do so, and assume or presume that someone later on will have to deal with the repercussions. It's an easy trap to fall into.

In any case, I'm not suggesting that the Drive.AI demise was due solely to the add-on kit aspects, as there were many other factors involved, yet I think it is worth a moment of reflection to consider how the driverless car developers are approaching their moonshot efforts, and what it means for the autonomous car emergence.

I'll also point out that there is an additional phenomenon that few are realizing is inevitably playing out and will impact the add-on kit dream, doing so as the ticking of the clock continues unabated.

Here's what it is (don't tell anyone).

Rather than overnight switching our stock of conventional cars to newly emerging fully autonomous cars, instead what is more likely is that we'll have lots of semi-autonomous cars enter into the marketplace. Thus, there will be old-time conventional cars with no or quite limited ADAS, there will be semi-autonomous or Level 3 cars with boosted ADAS, and then there will be the Level 4 and Level 5 more fully autonomous cars.

The question of trying to leap whole hog from the bottom tier, the conventional car, up to the vaunted autonomous car might be too hard to do but making the leap from a semi-autonomous to a fully autonomous could very well be closer and within reach. As such, the add-on kits could potentially aim at converting a semi-autonomous into a fully autonomous car, a lesser leap.

It is not though a no-brainer to get from a semi-autonomous to a fully autonomous car, thus do not be holding your breath on that hope. I'll cover more about such a jump or leap in later columns.

Goodbye to Drive.AI, and thanks for being a piece of the puzzle that is gradually, and I assert inexorably going to lead us to true autonomous cars. May you Rest In Peace (RIP), and yet from your ashes let's entrust that your efforts will continue to echo and inform, even though your day has now ended.

That's an epitaph that is intended to optimistically commemorate those valiant efforts and uplift spirits that as one smallish driverless car maker falls to the wayside, the rest will garner lessons learned and we can all be better informed accordingly.

CHAPTER 4

BOEING 737
EMERGENCY FLAW
AND
AI SELF-DRIVING CARS

CHAPTER 4

BOEING 737

EMERGENCY FLAW

AND

AI SELF-DRIVING CARS

Boeing is back in the news with a newly found flaw in the 737 system, sorry to say.

I've previously pointed out that the Boeing 737 MAX has provided some vital analogues to the self-driving driverless car realm, particularly involving design guffaws over sensors and their use in automatically taking on the driving task (see my posted piece on this).

In the now well-known Boeing 737 case that ended-up grounding their fleet, the Angle-Of-Attack (AOA) sensor became the focus of attention as to its inadequate software, unable to deal with sensor faults, and for its programming of being overly assertive in co-sharing the driving (piloting) efforts.

It is something that could readily happen in a somewhat akin manner to self-driving driverless cars.

For the case of semi-autonomous cars, such as Level 2 and Level 3, involving the co-sharing of the driving task by a human driver and the automation, there is a chance that the automation could attempt to outgun or outman the human driver, doing so erroneously.

Imagine you are trying to steer your car, doing so to the left, and meanwhile the automation is trying to also steer it, but steering hard to the right, you would be vexed and likely gravely endangered if zipping along on a freeway and making life-or-death driving choices.

The latest Boeing system error discovery is completely separate and instead focuses on an entirely different matter, namely an issue that could potentially arise during emergency procedures of a flight. It was found somewhat by happenstance, arising during simulator tests that were being done to try and overall gauge the readiness of the Boeing 737 to start flights again.

I'll stop right there for a moment and point out some salient aspects that this highlights:

- This latest found error has been hidden in the Boeing 737 all along and could have been encountered at any time (during the invocation of emergency procedures).

- The newly found error was discovered not by intent of trying to find it, but merely as a consequence of otherwise doing general and overall testing (via simulation).

- This added scrutiny and testing was done because of the sparked attention of the AOA sensor case, and likely might not have ever been overtly found, other than if an incident led to a crash and during the crash investigation this error was revealed and traced as the root of the cause.

What does that have to do with driverless autonomous cars?

Answer: The same kinds of "hidden" (unexposed) aspects could be lurking and awaiting deadly results in self-driving driverless cars.

In short, the driverless cars already on our public roadways might very well contain hidden errors (I'd say it is nearly a guarantee that they are in existence and not merely some slim chance), those driverless cars might get the green light for added expansion of use and yet still contain the latent error, and the error could remain undiscovered and only unmasked once (sadly, regrettably) a deadly car crash occurred involving the self-driving car.

Just thought I'd mention this as a forewarning and that we can use the Boeing matter as a harbinger of what might come next in the self-driving car realm.

More About The Latest Boeing 737 Bug

Let's further unpack the latest found Boeing 737 bug.

According to reports about the error, while invoking emergency procedures of a flight due to an awry stabilizer on the plane, if there is simultaneously a fault that occurs in the flight-control system, particularly a computer processor or chip that might have issues, the resulting impact is that the automation will apparently attempt to move the tail panel, causing the nose to aim downward.

It is said that a pilot in such a situation might be baffled and unaware of the automation moving the panel. Furthermore, the pilot might have a difficult time trying to sort out what the plane is doing, since the automation is working as a co-shared driver and yet the human pilot doesn't realize what their robotic companion is up to.

Keep in mind that all of this puzzling action would be occurring at the worst of times, when the plane is already in a dire state and the emergency procedures are being activated.

In that manner, the pilot is already under great stress, as opposed to say level flight and with nothing untoward happening, and thus the human pilot must contend with trying to keep the plane in air and safe, while simultaneously contending with the hidden bug (that the pilot doesn't know about).

It makes things a lot tougher on the human pilot and means that the error is essentially arising at the worst of times. The pilot is caught in the middle of real-time split second decision making, and their co-shared driver (the automation) is essentially working against them at that juncture.

Before I launch into some lessons to be learned for the development and use of self-driving cars, I'd like to stipulate that the actual aspects of the newly found bug are still being elaborated and so my aforementioned description is subject to change. Nonetheless, I think it is reasonable to guess that the error found so far has those overall characteristics and we can levelheadedly generalize to how this could apply to self-driving cars.

How This Applies To Self-Driving Cars

First, the aspect that the newly found bug relates to emergency procedures is rather significant for self-driving cars.

Much of the work today on self-driving cars tends to focus on the everyday aspects of the driving task.

Developers and testers are pretty much dealing with the driverless car being able to make left turns, right turns, go straight on a highway, and avoid obstacles and other cars. The roadway usage is likely nearly composed of commonplace driving conditions.

How often do you find yourself driving a car and suddenly being confronted with an emergency?

Well, I hope that you aren't finding yourself routinely involved in driving emergencies, which if you are then maybe you ought to do some reflection about why that might be (though, yes, if you drive an ambulance, a police car, or fire truck, I can certainly see why).

Anyway, my point is that the prevalence of "testing" of driverless cars on our roadways is barely touching upon what they might do during an emergency driving situation.

You could say the same about airplanes. By-and-large, airplanes are being flown in an everyday manner, which I'm not saying isn't still a hefty skill-based activity, but it is generally rare that planes end-up in emergency circumstances. What will a plane do during an emergency? If the software and systems haven't been well-tested for specifics about what occurs during emergencies, it could be anyone's guess as to what the plane might try to do.

Will a self-driving car do the "right thing" during an emergency driving situation?

The roadway tryouts probably aren't going to expose whether the automation is going to do something amiss or not. This applies not only to the fully autonomous cars, such as Level 4 and Level 5, but also applies to the Level 2 and Level 3 semi-autonomous cars too.

Here's then some further lessons to be learned:

- The roadway tryouts need to somehow encompass emergencies yet do so safely and in a carefully contained manner, which should be done on closed tracks or providing grounds, rather than on our public streets.

- Simulations of driverless cars need to especially tackle and exercise the emergency procedure aspects of self-driving cars, which otherwise could be neglected or not given proper attention.

- Automakers and tech firms would be wise to not wait until someone somewhere gets into a deadly crash involving a self-driving car and for which later on belatedly it is found out that an emergency procedure in the system had a lurking flaw. Give priority now, not after-the-fact.

- We must also all accept the notion that no matter how much simulation you do, and no matter how much roadway tryouts you undertake, there is still a chance of bugs or errors inside any complex system such as the AI running self-driving cars.

That doesn't though excuse anyone from doing exhaustive and in-depth testing, since you cannot simply say that well, because those bugs or errors are hard to find, just give up trying.

Ultimately, the odds are that the automakers and tech firms will be held accountable, in at least a court of law, if not the court of public opinion, over how extensively they tested their systems and what they did to try and prevent bugs or errors and what they did to find them and correct them.

Conclusion

I've once again tried to use the Boeing 737 as a handy means of shedding light on self-driving driverless cars, doing so to gain added awareness for the advent of semi-autonomous and fully autonomous cars.

An especially disconcerting aspect about the Boeing aspect is that airplane and flight readiness testing consists of quite rigorous assessment methods and most would say is topnotch, yet if it can let such an error or flaw slip under the testing radar, imagine what is happening in the self-driving driverless car realm, which tends to be less thorough and right now more so rushed to meet get-it-on-the-road deadlines.

Pause for a thought on that point.

Overall, it is instructive to take the headlines of today and try to see how they apply to driverless cars. This just might avoid adverse headlines of the future that could castigate the failures or missteps of autonomous car designers and makers that should have been doing proper and needed efforts before bad things happened.

CHAPTER 5
SPINOUT TESLA AUTOPILOT
AND
AI SELF-DRIVING CARS

CHAPTER 5

SPINOUT TESLA AUTOPILOT

AND

AI SELF-DRIVING CARS

Tesla continues to be in the news as their latest counts of (especially) Model 3 car deliveries are reported and analyzed with intense interest.

The media seems to vacillate at times from wringing its hands about whether Tesla is a customer demand story versus an automobile production story, either not having sufficient demand for their autos or having the demand but stuck in a sort of production purgatory trying to get their vaunted cars into the hands of consumers wanting one.

Some lament that it is unfair and inappropriate to keep Tesla in the "prove it" box continuously, forcing the company to each quarter provide adequate proof that it deserves to be in business and that it will continue to remain in business. Daily swings of the stock price and weekly news flashes generally dominate the attention that the firm seems to get.

I tend to find insightful this comment uttered recently by a Morgan Stanley analyst that said this: "We continue to believe Tesla is fundamentally overvalued, but potentially strategically undervalued."

Some were quite puzzled by the remark. Is it perhaps a riddle of the Sphinx? Was the analyst speaking in tongues? Maybe it is one of those Zen-like kinds of expressions that gradually makes sense if you let your mind fly free.

It struck me as rather straightforward and pointed, I believe.

Parsing the statement closely, it seems to me that there are elements of Tesla that are like grapes on the vine, having a huge upside strategic potential of ripening and producing possibly a rare and very enticing wine.

That wine doesn't yet exist, though, so you can't readily embody it into the value today of the firm, since there's a chance that those grapes won't bear fruit.

One could assert that there is an overvaluation taking place by the marketplace today, based on what we can see and touch right now, meanwhile, further down-the-road, there could be a strategic blossoming of those grapes, producing tremendous added value at that time. Thus, there is simultaneously a moment-to-moment overvaluing at this time, and yet there is a longer-term undervaluing of what might emerge.

It's one of those calculated risks and probabilities occasions.

In particular, let's consider their self-driving tech as the grapes on the vine.

I'd like to discuss these three major topics thereof:

1) Valuing the self-driving tech
2) Where the value arises from
3) Timing aspects impacting estimated value

Valuing The Self-Driving Tech

Using Morgan Stanley's estimates, it is suggested that the value of the Tesla self-driving tech side of the firm accounts for about one-fifth of the total market cap of the company, which at a market cap of $42B led them to arrive broadly at a number of $8.5B for the self-driving tech portion.

Some industry watchers have previously indicated that they believe that Cruise, a self-driving car company now part of GM, might be worth around $15B.

This makes one wonder whether the estimated $8.5B valuation about Tesla's self-driving car tech might be low in comparison to the $15B for Cruise, depending upon how you compare Cruise's self-driving tech versus Tesla's self-driving tech efforts.

Maybe, one could argue that the Tesla number ought to be higher. Perhaps nearly doubling toward being assessed at the $15B mark.

Let's next consider what some suggest might be a valuation of praised self-driving tech bellwether Waymo (Google/Alphabet's entity).

Considered by most to be the top dog of self-driving tech, a few years ago there were suggestions that Waymo might be worth $4.5B, and nowadays some are floating a gargantuan number of $175B. Once again, we need to decide whether trying to compare Tesla's self-driving tech to Waymo's self-driving tech is an apple to apples comparison, or whether it is more akin to an apple to oranges comparison.

Elon Musk famously expressed that he believes Tesla is headed toward a total market cap of $500B.

If you use the notion that the self-driving tech at Tesla can be attributed to one-fifth of the company's total value, this means that the Tesla self-driving tech is worth around $100B, putting it into the league of the Waymo suggested valuation of $175B.

And so, we are left with the aspect that either Tesla's self-driving tech is to be valued at around $8.5B, or whether it should be closer to around $15B (but in that case the self-driving tech would leap to being considered nearly 40% of the existing market cap), or might be amazingly $100B (if you buy into the belief that Tesla's self-driving tech can reach true autonomous capability).

Part of the difficulty in trying to figure out the worth question involves whether or not the Tesla self-driving tech is going to achieve true autonomous capability or not.

That's where the value will arise from.

Where The Value Rises From

As I've mentioned in prior columns, and especially after seeing their Tesla Autonomy Investor Day, we can't really yet say for sure whether Tesla is heading forthrightly towards achieving true full autonomous car capabilities, considered Level 4 and Level 5, and still has only shown an indication of Level 2 and Level 3.

The showcase at the Investor Day was lacking in revealing anything substantive to provide actual evidence of Level 4 and Level 5, and unfortunately laid out what non-experts might think appeared to be highly technical and yet was merely some rather tech-simplistic self-driving car Lecture 101 depictions.

Will the grapes on the vines ripen or not?

At this time, you can't say for sure they will.

Thus, we really cannot reasonably argue in any practical way about whether Tesla's self-driving tech should be valued at $8.5B, or $15B, or at $100B. So far, Tesla continues to hold their cards hidden from view.

Are they holding aces and have the royal flush, or do they have a smattering of odds-and-ends cards and maybe can at best bring together a lowly pair or a three of-a-kind?

If you could get a peek at their cards, you'd have a better chance of assessing what they are holding.

Imagine if Tesla was willing to spin-out their self-driving tech, either making it a wholly owned entity that could seek other customers beyond Tesla, or perhaps make it a distinct entity for which others could invest in or sell it outright to someone else (or, there's the idea too that some have suggested, namely break-up the firm and splay various portions into their own entities).

Any of those approaches would generally mean that the cards they are holding would need to be shown to someone other than themselves.

Were there substantive indication of being able to achieve true autonomous capability, this would make such an entity likely eagerly sought by others that are struggling to get to Level 4 and Level 5, or possibly be rather attractive to firms that have been sitting on the sidelines that might want to leapfrog to the front of the pack on self-driving cars.

Some argue that Musk would not want to give up control over the golden goose, the self-driving tech.

One supposes that an arrangement could still be made for him to continue to have substantive control, plus in any case it would seem the case that Tesla would still need the self-driving tech and thus would have to retain an ability to use it or license it from the entity.

Likewise, the entity could potentially license its self-driving tech to a multitude of customers, rather than being captive to only one.

For those that point out that it would potentially make Tesla's become a me-too if their self-driving tech was spread around to others, this could be dealt with by having for example a delayed aspect to the release of new features. Tesla might get the first dibs on new releases and have a market window during which those could not be provided to competing automakers.

There are some that argue that the self-driving tech efforts might weaken or dilute if they aren't fully within the Tesla sphere and fully under Musk's direction. The other side of that coin is that some suggest the self-driving tech would be more likely to gain by no longer being strictly at the behest of Musk and could perhaps pursue avenues that have been heretofore considered off-limits or perceived by Musk as worthy of pursuit.

Unbundling Of the Self-Driving Tech

In contemplating their self-driving tech, you could somewhat unbundle the self-driving tech elements.

Consider these crucial aspects of any self-driving tech portfolio:
a) Data of actual roadway driving efforts (useful for Machine Learning)
b) Source code of self-driving software and systems
c) Hardware for self-driving tech
d) Patents and Intellectual Property (IP) of self-driving tech
e) AI developers for self-driving tech advancement

I'll briefly walk you through each of those elements.

Let's start with what appears to be the most significant and unique element that they possess.

There's the vast trove of collected roadway data that Tesla claims they have amassed via their sensors on the Tesla's, which could be significantly valuable for Machine Learning and advancing self-driving tech.

Presumably, this is a richness of data unlike what anyone else has in-hand.

Within that massive data set are presumably a multitude of edge cases, which consist of the tougher to contend with corner or edge aspects of driving situations, a potential stumbling block towards getting to Level 4 and Level 5. By leveraging the dataset, you'd able to more readily train self-driving tech to deal with the somewhat intractable "last mile" toward full driving autonomy.

The data presumably is also cross-representative of driving situations across the entire United States.

This is important in that many of the other self-driving tech efforts are focused on specific locales, such as say Phoenix or Silicon Valley, but have not yet made demonstrative forays into other parts of the country where the roadway conditions differ, and where the weather conditions differ, and where drivers at times might exhibit different driving behaviors, etc.

The data also presumably contains international driving. This is another open front for the automakers and tech firms that ultimately want their self-driving cars to be workable beyond the borders of the United States, opening up global opportunities to sell and use their driverless cars.

The rub is that we don't know that Tesla really has this data, we don't know what shape it is in, and so on.

Part of the hidden hand of poker cards.

Looking beyond the data aspects, which as mentioned seems to be their most distinctive and unique aspect of their self-driving tech portfolio, there's the hardware such as their now home-grown FSD (so-called Full Self-Driving) processor, which might have value to others but definitely has fierce competition, and then there's the software of their Autopilot.

The software might be in great shape and ready for reuse in other vehicles of differing brands and models. Or, the software might be a tangled web of spaghetti, for which it only works on Tesla's, and cannot be ported or used without extensive and costly unwinding and reverse engineering. If that were the case, it would certainly diminish the value aspects of the software.

There's the patents and IP that Tesla has, allowing for not simply using the self-driving tech, but could be leveraged for going after other self-driving tech makers and users.

I know it seems disgusting to some, yet in theory there is a possibility of making money by being a patent troll in self-driving tech. This spin-out or sold-off entity that we're pretending might exist with the Tesla self-driving tech could decide to go on the pursuit of others that are developing self-driving tech, and get them to pony up if there is potential infringement, or seek the courts to get renumeration from those violated patents.

There's the acqui-hire possibility too. In today's hot AI world, firms often buy a company to mainly get the AI talent, the AI developers, systems designers, coders, testers, and the like. The tech that the acquired firm had developed is sometimes put aside, or partially reused, and not considered especially significant when doing the acquisition, since it's the team of experienced AI rock-stars that the acquiring firms wants to grab ahold of.

Timing Aspects Impacting Estimated Value

I'll finish up this discussion by emphasizing that timing is everything.

As an example, here's two ways in which timing could undermine the valuation of the self-driving tech:

i.   The self-driving tech ends-up leading to car accidents and injuries or deaths

ii. The self-driving tech is too far behind and others eclipse it to Level 4 and Level 5

In the business of self-driving tech, if the tech contributes toward a car accident involving injuries or deaths, which of course no one hopes will happen, but we know that it can and has happened, there is the potential for a reputational diminishment and tarnishing that could wipe out the value of the self-driving tech.

It can be a long climb out of the self-driving tech abyss to later on try and recapture the brand and get others to believe that the system is safe and sound. During that period, rightly or wrongly, the self-driving tech will be at rock bottom of being perceived as worthwhile and valuable.

The other example of timing involves taking longer to get to the desired Level 4 and Level 5 than others.

In this moonshot race, if others are able to achieve Level 4 and Level 5 first, some believe that it will make other efforts that are not yet there to become perceived as lackluster. Though this might be unfair, and you could potentially argue that the efforts that are "lagging" behind the front pack might actually turn out to be better in some respects, the impetus is bound to falter for anyone painted as second run.

In short, if the self-driving tech is too late to the party, you can anticipate that it will take a big ding and dent in terms of valuation. The pizzazz will be gone.

Conclusion

For now, the Tesla self-driving tech is locked away inside of Tesla and there's not yet any viable means to ascertain the value as it relates to achieving true autonomy.

Piece by piece, you can make the case that either as a bundle or even unbundled, the value could exist.

There is the potential for amazing value, yet the clock is also ticking, and time will either harm or propel the value.

It is said that wine improves with age, but currently the grapes are still on the vine and we don't know if the resultant wine will be incredibly sweet and savory, or it might turn out to be moldy and undrinkable.

CHAPTER 6

EARTHQUAKES
AND
AI SELF-DRIVING CARS

CHAPTER 6

EARTHQUAKES

AND

AI SELF-DRIVING CARS

California has been rocking and rolling, doing so to the tune of several recent earthquakes and aftershocks. That shaking feeling has also been felt in numerous nearby states, along with finding its way south of the border into Mexico.

Fortunately, this round of earth movements has not led to massive destruction and perhaps serves somewhat helpfully as a wake-up call for earthquake preparedness efforts for when the big one actually hits.

One aspect that many people don't consider involves the roadway disruption that an earthquake can potentially produce.

Sure, we all tend to think about our homes swaying and the dangers of household objects falling upon us, or maybe you might be imagining how stores could dump over their racks of groceries and goods, but do you ponder the adverse impact to the streets and highways.

Consider Earthquake Impacts To Our Roads

As soon as an earthquake has made itself known, you might be surprised to know that phalanxes of inspectors and others trained to examine roadway cracks and gaps are on-the-go, fanning out to check the transportation infrastructure (this is standard operating procedure in cities that are earthquake savvy).

The assessments are especially focused on bridges, overpasses, and other similar structures that could be expected to falter or fail when the earth provides a sharp jolt of energy.

Meanwhile, people that have cars are frequently desirous of using their cars fairly soon after an earthquake occurs.

People often react to an earthquake by worrying about loved ones that might be a distance away and so will jump into their cars to race over to be with a relative or close friend. Or, sometimes the destruction where you are is so overwhelming that you opt to drive out of the damaged area to find a locale that was untouched or at least still fully operating.

The thing is that if you want to use your car after an earthquake has happened, you don't know for sure that you can drive to wherever you might want to go.

The roads could be unpassable, or dangerous to drive on.

Even recently here in California there was a small town that was pretty much cut-off from outsiders due to a lone stretch of highway that fed into the town and due to earthquake damage became nearly impossible to drive on.

This raises an interesting question, namely what would self-driving driverless cars do if they were faced with driving in an area that was experiencing an earthquake?

Let's unpack that question.

Dealing With Earthquakes And Driving

There are two major elements to consider about driving and earthquakes, consisting firstly about what happens when driving during an earthquake, and the other aspect involves trying to drive after an earthquake has subsided.

In my own personal experience, I've been driving my car during earthquakes and also shortly after an earthquake has completed.

Luckily, my active earthquake driving was generally undetectable in the driver's seat, being so mild in impacting the motion of the car that I tended not to even realize an earthquake was taking place (it was when the radio announcer began to exclaim that an earthquake was underway that I realized something was afoot).

Unless you are really close to the main shoving action of the earthquake, your car is probably not going to be pushed around per se by the shaking earth.

Usually, you'll see nearby billboards or signposts that seem to be swaying back-and-forth, or you might see an overpass shimmering a bit as you go underneath it.

The roadway itself is bound to be the most pronounced indicator of the earthquake taking place.

Cracks can suddenly appear and gaps in the road might loom as though some unseen force has opted to make use of a holepunch. You can also likely see debris that is falling from any high rising structures adjacent to the roadway. If there are trees overhanging to the street that you are on, the tree limbs and branches can begin plopping onto the asphalt in front of your car.

Of course, the impact that you'll witness is dependent upon the severity of the earthquake, including how far away the earthquake epicenter was. If you are quite close to the main burst of earth moving action, the odds of heightened damages and dangers goes up.

Power lines could fall onto the roadway, and entire building structures could completely fall and land on cars or block the paths of cars.

Often times the reactions of the other drivers is more worrisome than the effects of the earthquake itself.

Drivers can suddenly start swerving their cars, perhaps jamming unexpectedly on their brakes. Some drivers go into a pure panic mode. They aren't sure whether they should keep going, or come to an immediate halt, or pull over to the side of the road, and tend to lose their minds about watching for other traffic. It's possible to become so transfixed with trying to avoid those newly formed cracks and debris that drivers fail to consider the other cars that are on the roadway with them.

It becomes a dog-eat-dog world. I'll drive to save myself, each driver thinks, and those other drivers ought to be doing the same.

Suppose a self-driving driverless car was on the roadway during an earthquake.

In theory, a driverless car that was already able to drive on everyday streets would presumably have capabilities to detect aspects such as cracks in the road, debris on the roadway, and so on. As such, you could likely expect that the autonomous car would be able to cope with the appearance of these traffic hazards.

Furthermore, the antics of the other drivers would also be something that the driverless car should be able to contend with. As you know, human drivers can perform all sorts of oddball maneuvers at any time, and so the driverless car is hopefully ready for how the earthquake frantic human drivers might be reacting.

Would the driverless car realize that an earthquake was underway?

I'd say that the emerging crop of autonomous cars would be utterly clueless that an earthquake is taking place.

Driverless Cars Not Earthquake Aware

Unlike a human driver, these driverless cars have no commonsense reasoning and are lacking in any intelligent behavior.

The self-driving AI systems would be merely reacting to whatever occurs around or nearby to the driverless car, as detected via the sensors such as on-board cameras, radar, ultrasonic, LIDAR, and so on.

Don't expect the AI to have any idea that an earthquake is the underlying cause for the sudden appearance of roadway blockages and the driver antics that might be occurring. Instead, the AI would be simply reacting to whatever happens to appear as it so appears.

At some juncture, the AI might decide that there is so much untoward activity on the road that the driverless car should pull over to the side of the roadway. If you were a passenger inside such a driverless car, I'm sure you would be yelling at the AI to take proper evasive action and perhaps be pleading with it to pullover, though depending upon how good the Natural Language Processing (NLP) might be, the AI might be ignore your pleas and have no realization of what you are requesting.

Some are expecting that the early versions of driverless cars will have an OnStar-like capability to allow you as a passenger to seek out the assistance of a human remote operator. Assuming that the electronic communications is still functioning during the quake, you could potentially get a human agent on the horn and ask them to get the AI to pullover.

Many AI developers would argue that an earthquake is a pretty rare event and thus having to code the driverless car to specifically deal with a quake is not worthwhile at this time. Driverless car earthquake preparedness would be considered an edge or corner case. At some point in the future, once the core capabilities of autonomous cars have been dealt with, those edge or corner cases would then be taken into account.

Anyone stuck inside a driverless car during an earthquake might not be so sympathetic that postponing the earthquake handling capability was a futuristic edge case of lesser importance.

Add to this notion that if the driverless car had only children in it, and no adult present, the situation could be rather problematic.

Post-Earthquake Driving

After an earthquake has taken its toll, the act of driving has a multitude of facets to be considered.

There is the chance that online maps would be updated with the status of roadways such that a driverless car would be informed about what places are still passable and which ones should be avoided. As such, the AI routing would presumably attempt to drive only where it is safest to do so. Seems like a good thing.

One question will be whether you as a human passenger in a driverless car can override what the AI wants to do.

Suppose that your elderly father is at home and his neighborhood was struck hard by the earthquake. Assume that roadway inspectors have declared that no one should be using the roads in that neighborhood.

The AI system has picked-up the "don't drive there" status and therefore refuses to drive in that area.

Meanwhile, you are willing to take a chance to drive there, hoping to reach your father, though the driverless car won't proceed and there aren't any driving controls for you to use to commandeer the self-driving car.

Should you be able to insist to the AI that it must drive you in an area that otherwise has been declared as verboten to drive in?

The same can be said for first responders that might be trying to reach areas to provide food supplies or render medical aid. Again, keep in mind that the AI has no commonsense reasoning and therefore won't be able to somehow discuss the matter.

If a driverless car does cart you around after an earthquake, one potential advantage it might have over human drivers and conventional cars is the ability to communicate via V2V (vehicle-to-vehicle) electronic communications. Other driverless cars can be sharing roadway status in real-time with each other, letting others nearby know that a crack can be avoided by taking a different route or alerting other autonomous cars to avoid a pole that's fallen onto the roadway.

It is also anticipated that we'll have V2I (vehicle-to-infrastructure) electronic communications, allowing the roads and transportation infrastructure to directly provide status to driverless cars. A bridge might be able to send a message to a nearing autonomous car to warn about which lanes are safe and which ones are not. Edge computing devices along a stretch of highway can be conveying to a stream of driverless cars the most up-to-date indications about the road status.

Conclusion

For those of you that don't live in an earthquake prone area, you might be tempted to consider the driverless car and earthquakes issues as inapplicable to you.

I'd suggest you perhaps reconsider the matter by contemplating what other kinds of natural disasters might be prevalent in your part of the country.

Hurricanes?

Twisters?

Whatever you might have, you can recast my earlier points about earthquakes into the realm of your own local kinds of natural disasters.

Driverless cars are going to initially be as clueless about earthquake related driving as they will be about hurricane driving (both during one and post-damage), tornado driving, etc. In that case, we are all going to be in the same boat, as it were, having to deal with an AI system that won't comprehend the impacts of a natural disaster. That could be disastrous in some cases.

CHAPTER 7

FORD MOBILITY LAB

AND

AI SELF-DRIVING CARS

CHAPTER 7

FORD MOBILITY LAB

AND

AI SELF-DRIVING CARS

Imagine this. A self-driving car is whisking brother and sister youngsters over to their elementary school, doing so while the in-car AI-based tutoring system is interactively getting them prepped for their classes that day. Zipping past the smart car is a petite sized autonomous delivery vehicle, carrying prescribed medicine from the local pharmacy to their grandmother at home, she had helped the kids get dressed that morning and didn't have time to go out to get her needed meds.

Pedestrians walking along on the sidewalk nearby and hoping to cross the street have been receiving text messages to their smartphones notifying them to stay out of the roadway until it is clear for crossing. Traffic lights meanwhile were beaming out special electronic signals aiming to balance the flow of traffic in this area and communicating directly with the cars and pedestrians to efficiently guide them and keep them safely out of harm's way, using V2I (vehicle-to-infrastructure) and V2P (vehicle-to-pedestrian) transmissions.

This futuristic scenario is going to become daily reality at a real place in an existing Detroit locale called Corktown, selected as part of a major initiative that's being spearheaded by Ford.

Considered to be Detroit's oldest neighborhood, the Corktown area is being reimagined and revitalized to become a showcase urban setting that seamlessly leverages advanced mobility capabilities. With the active participation of a myriad of key stakeholders, including city and state regulators, businesses, colleges, engineers, AI developers, and the like, Ford is aiming to collaboratively create a living lab of mobility that can explore how real people in real cities can best leverage the latest in mobility solutions.

Indeed, as the overall renaissance of Detroit takes place, one of the perhaps most illuminating and transformative efforts will be this innovative mobility corridor involving Corktown.

As a microcosm of how the future of mobility might well be smartly designed and astutely emerge among us, this groundbreaking initiative provides a vital signpost for city and neighborhood planners everywhere and will demonstrate in a practical everyday way how people and tech-advancing mobility options will best blend and enable the transport of us all, including too those today that might be mobility marginalized.

I recently had an opportunity to speak with Dr. Ken Washington, Ford's CTO and VP of Research & Advanced Engineering, doing so at the TC Sessions: Mobility summit held in San Jose, California on July 10, 2019, and we discussed the Corktown overarching vision and approach.

Let's unpack what this pioneering initiative is all about.

The Big Picture Being Envisioned

First, as readers of my column know, I have extolled many times that the advent of autonomous driverless cars will be a massive form of "change agent" which will spark and activate many other changes in how we travel, where we go, how we get there, along with a restructuring of the landscape of our lives.

Most roadway tryout efforts today that are aimed at adopting self-driving cars are being done in a rather isolated and disconnected drop-it-in manner.

Driverless cars are essentially being substituted for conventional human driven cars as though it is a simple one-for-one swap. The surrounding environs are as they exist today, absent of other upcoming advances in micro-mobility such as e-scooters, e-bikes, e-skateboards, etc. There's no interconnectedness being tried out with these mobile forms of transport and nor with the traffic lights and roadway status systems, and there's decidedly no effort to immerse pedestrians into what will soon enough become a networked transportation-aware ecosystem.

This belies the true likely impacts of how autonomous cars and other new mobility advances will ultimately enter into and spark a reshaping of our society.

Two of my rules-of-thumb about driverless cars are:
- A self-driving car must not be an island unto itself
- It takes a village to design and deploy autonomous cars

We need to look ahead and seek to coordinate and integrate what otherwise could easily become a morass of disparate mobility options. It is important to anticipate the interactions needed among multiple modes of mobility, along with how us humans will use and gain from the advanced tech being devised and deployed.

That's where Corktown comes into the picture.

The idea is to insightfully and collaboratively enhance an entire locale that can be a testbed for the latest in mobility.

You could do this in an artificial manner at a closed track or proving ground, but it would lack a sense of realism and be unlikely to reveal the day-to-day dynamics of what really works and what doesn't.

In a bold manner, it would be better to work with an area that is desirous of being revitalized and get a twofer by not only aiding the rebirth of the neighborhood but also dovetail advances in mobility at the same time. This is an overtly conceived urban-favorable experiment that will be a win-win in many significant ways.

A cornerstone of the Corktown effort involves the rehab of a cherished Detroit landmark, Michigan Central Station, a former train station that Ford acquired last year and has committed to spending several hundred million dollars to reconstitute into a centerpiece for the innovation hub.

Creating A Vibrant Mobility Living Lab

Ken explained that the Corktown setting will consist of about 1.2 million square feet encompassing the already being revamped Michigan Central Station and a number of nearby properties that were acquired and are also being revitalized or reconstituted (properties such as an old public-school book depository, a brass factory, a hosiery factory, and so on).

This all will now become a modern-day mix of office space, up-to-date retail establishments, contemporary housing, community meeting sites, open spaces for parks, and other new developments.

Besides establishing these new properties, the notion is to ensure that there is an entire community of people that will be living, working, and playing in a dynamic neighborhood, primed to explore state-of-the-art transportation mechanisms and provide feedback about how it is meshing together.

Envision entrepreneurs, artists, scientists, teachers, government workers, doctors, baristas, and everyone of all walks of life being able to actively participate in a living lab that is trying to explore new mobility modes, doing so while everyday life is happening, and yet at the same time being able to share their feedback and then watch and respond as adjustments occur accordingly.

As Ken keenly explained, this Corktown revitalization will illuminate and test mobility of the future, creating tomorrow together, doing so in an energizing way and hand-in-hand with the community.

When the Corktown initiative was initially announced, Ford had also predicted that about 5,000 new jobs would be created in the area, of which about half from Ford and the other half by the numerous business partners aiding in making a go of the mobility living lab. Already there are many of these new jobs arising in the venue.

Conclusion

The driverless car industry needs a place where mobility is built into the DNA of the community and can allow for open exploration of emerging new tech, and do so in a real-world setting that involves the messiness and unexpectedness that comes with real people trying to go about their hectic lives.

Autonomous car startups don't have the kind of clout or resources to tackle a community wide, interconnected, roadway sharing, pedestrian involved, eclectic kind of environment.

That's where a major automotive firm like Ford can leverage its size and brand strength, bringing together the varied set of stakeholders that would need to be enjoined into such an effort and spurring them into believing in the possibilities of an endeavor of this magnitude.

As Ken and I discussed, there are some mobility developers and engineers that carp that mobility is arduous to design and implement because people make the problem hard, well, there's no point in sticking your head into the sand about it, and instead we'll all be better off to have people be part of the mobility systems development life cycle, ensuring that afoul mobility options are expunged and that appropriate mobility options are discovered and extended.

Corktown, listed in the National Registry of Historic Places and revered for its historical significance, now stands at the forefront of making essential contributions to the future of Auto 2.0, and can foster mobility advances in a practical and usable way that every city USA and globally can gain from.

Keep your eye on Corktown.

CHAPTER 8

APOLLO 11 ERROR CODE

AND

AI SELF-DRIVING CARS

CHAPTER 8

APOLLO 11 ERROR CODE

AND

AI SELF-DRIVING CARS

The 50th anniversary of the historic Apollo 11 landing on the moon will be taking place on July 20, 2019.

You might recall the famous utterance heard worldwide that the Eagle had landed (the word "Eagle" was the name given to the lunar module aka lunar lander used in the Apollo 11 mission).

Going back in time to that incredible feat that occurred on July 20, 1969, you might want to listen carefully to the audio chatter between astronauts Neil Armstrong and Buzz Aldrin while carrying on a dialogue with the mission control center during the descent to the moon.

Unless you are a nerdish fan of either computers or spaceflight, you might not have noticed that there was a subtle undercurrent of concern about some rather jarring alarm-blaring display-flashing error codes known as the numbers 1202 and the 1201.

It's an incredible story that the general public knows little about.

Let's unpack the tense tale, along with considering lessons learned that can be applied to the now emerging self-driving driverless autonomous cars.

Anxious Moments During The First Landing On The Moon

The lunar module that was being piloted down to the moon surface began to report errors when the craft was just seven and a half minutes away from landing.

Think about this for a moment. I assure you that having errors crop-up while in the midst of such an already tricky and risky effort is not something you desire to occur. It was later indicated that the heart rates for both the astronauts jumped up feverishly when the errors began to appear.

Things were tense, especially since landing on the moon had never actually occurred before and had only been practiced in a simulator.

The astronauts were faced with the possibility that they might need to call-off the landing if something went awry during the descent. If they didn't land on the first try, there was no second try available and they'd have to sheepishly and disappointingly return to earth without having landed on the moon.

It would have been a crushing blow to NASA, it would have been a heart wrenching let-down for the USA, it would have potentially tarnished the image of America worldwide, along with creating an expanded time window for the Russians to try and get to a moon landing before the United States did.

Everything was on the line.

Of course, worse still would have been a crash landing onto the moon, which one shudders to even contemplate.

Two obscure error codes were being displayed, each consisting of four digits, and represented status that there was an issue or problem occurring in their spacecraft.

During the design of the system for the lunar lander, the developers had come up with a slew of error codes that could be displayed if the computer detected something amiss on the craft.

Here's the rub. When the astronauts had done simulated landings, doing so over and over again, not all of the possible error codes were tested out, and thus there was some error codes that the astronauts had never seen or directly knew about.

As luck or unluck would have it, the two error codes of 1202 and 1201 had not been previously exhibited during their training efforts. As such, the astronauts were unaware of what those particular error codes signified. Furthermore, even most of the mission control staff monitoring the landing had not seen the 1202 and 1201 before either.

Okay, let's try to relive history, if you will.

Put yourself into the cramped lunar module. With just minutes left to land, bells start ringing and buttons are flashing, trying to get your rapt attention. Nearly immediately, the astronauts realized they didn't know what the error code signified, and so they (remarkedly) calmly brought it to the attention of mission control:

"It's a 1202."

Within mission control, there were blank stares as by-and-large no one knew what the 1202 was about. Meanwhile, Steve Bales, a guidance officer, called over to a backroom area where various engineers were stationed and ready to dig into any system related matter that might arise.

"1202. What's that?" he reportedly asked.

John "Jack" Garman, a NASA engineer, took a look at a list he had handmade of the numerous error codes that the teams had come up with.

He realized that the 1202 was a code meaning that the guidance computer on-board the landing craft was getting overloaded with tasks. The programmers had anticipated this overloading might someday occur, and so had established a system internal aspect that would automatically do a fast reboot and then a memory restore to try and get the computer back underway.

In theory, the computer was going to be able to resolve the error, without needing any human intervention. Garman said afterward that he figured if the 1202 error code didn't recur frequently during the rest of the descent, the astronauts were probably okay to proceed in spite of whatever was seemingly overloading the on-board computer system.

"Give us a reading on the 1202 program alarm," Neil said.

In the recorded voice transmissions, you can hear in Neil's voice a seriousness and sternness and exasperation that so far no one from mission control had yet told the astronauts what to do about the error.

Again, place yourself in the lunar module and imagine that you've got this crazy unknown 1202 error code screaming at you, you've never seen it before, you don't have any procedure in-hand to deal with it, and it could be something extremely dangerous, happening in real-time, while you are aiming to hopefully safely land on the moon, and you are completely in-the-dark as to what it is and what you are supposed to be doing about it.

Each second that the 1202 remains an unknown could be another second toward your doom.

Within mission control, Darmon and Bales relayed internally that the astronauts should proceed on the landing, and so capcom Charlie Duke said to the astronauts:

"We're go on that alarm."

In this context, "go" means that the landing could continue to proceed unabated. Also, since no further instruction of what to do was being voiced to the astronauts, it implied that the alarm, whatever it meant, could be ignored. If you are wondering whether the astronauts might have been curious about what the 1202 represented, I believe they only cared at the moment about whether the 1202 required any action on their part.

I was fortunate to have had lunch with Buzz Aldrin during a recent visit he made to Los Angeles, and when I asked him about the 1202, he indicated indeed that once mission control essentially said to not worry about it, he let it go and didn't put any further thought towards it.

This makes sense too, namely that no additional explanation or elaboration was particularly needed per se, plus the astronauts already had their hands full with trying to land, so they set aside worries about the 1202 and focused on the landing process.

If you listen to the remaining minutes of the recorded audio, you'll hear that the 1202 error happened again, and again, along with a related error code of the 1201. Mission control informed the astronauts that it was considered the same type of error and implied therefore that there was no need to do anything about the alarms.

For everyone listening at the time of the actual moon landing, the chatter seemed to be the normal kind of interaction you'd expect between the astronauts and mission control, often technical in nature and you don't really know what their jargon means or signifies.

In this case, it was a subplot of grave concern and intensity, but that millions upon millions of people listening were unaware was playing out in real-time and could have ditched the landing entirely.

That's the story within the story about the Apollo 11 moon landing.

Lessons Learned For Self-Driving Driverless Cars

Can a systems related matter that happened some fifty years ago be of relevance today?

Absolutely.

Self-driving driverless cars are real-time based systems that need to act quickly and drive a car while the vehicle is in-motion, perhaps on a freeway and barreling along at 70 miles per hour.

On-board the autonomous car are numerous computer processors, including various systems memory banks used to house programs that are being executed or performed to drive the car. In addition, there is a myriad of sensors on the car, such as cameras, radar, ultrasonic devices, LIDAR, and the like, all of which are collecting data during the driving act and relaying that data into the computer processors and memory banks.

In the case of the 1202 error on the Eagle, what prompted the error was (in simple terms) a faulty radar unit that was essentially bombarding the on-board computer in such a manner that the computer kept getting handed task after task, though the flooding tasks weren't truly needed to be undertaken. The Operating System (OS) of the computer allowed the memory to fill-up, but then this meant that other legitimate tasks would not have a slot to work in.

As I had mentioned earlier, the programmers had anticipated that somehow for whatever reason there might be a time when the on-board computer might become overloaded with tasks. They had devised an internal mechanism that if something untoward led to the memory getting maxed out, the system would do a fast reboot and memory reload, which hopefully would clear out whatever was causing the initial problem.

Though this does suggest that the computer can then proceed with the high priority of running the craft, notice that it does not necessarily solve the underlying problem of the radar unit that's pounding away at the computer.

In any case, the good news is that the trick of the quick reboot was able to deal with the matter and the other precious landing subsystems were able to do their thing, meanwhile the radar was continuing to be an irritant but not so much that it led the craft astray.

How many times have you rebooted your smartphone or laptop computer and then had it clear up a problem?

I'm betting you've done these many times.

Have you also perchance done a reboot and then later on the same problem seems to crop-up?

That's a somewhat similar case of the 1202, namely that the reboot temporarily "solves" the problem of letting the computer proceed, but it didn't "solve" the root cause of the faulty radar unit aspects.

Here then are some insightful lessons for AI developers, automakers, and tech firms that are creating the software and systems for driverless cars:

- **Anticipate and code for wayward sensors.** You cannot assume that the sensors on the driverless car will be working flawlessly. Besides the obvious aspect that the sensor might get blinded by dirt or debris, there is also the chance that the sensor could go berserk due to some internal bug or issue. Make sure to code for this possibility and have some provision of what to do once the matter arises.

- **Ensure that the driverless car OS is robust.** Some of the operating systems being used for autonomous cars are somewhat stripped down for speed, yet they need to also be able to handle a wide variety of both known and unpredictable faults or systems issues that could happen. Make sure the OS is up to the task of supporting the systems involved in driving the car, safely so.

- **Do not ignore edge cases.** The focus for most driverless car efforts right now is aiming at driving during normal everyday conditions, and not dealing with unusual or infrequent kinds of driving situations (so-called "edge" aspects). This though belies the true aspects of driving which can include foul weather, bad roadways, and the like. Autonomous cars that are being tried out on our public streets need to be ready to handle edge or corner cases.

- **Testing must be exhaustive.** If you leave out test cases when testing a driverless car, you are setting up a potentially dangerous situation that someday in the real-world the thing you didn't test will happen, and perhaps have quite adverse consequences. Testing needs to be as complete as feasible.

- **Use reboots cautiously and only as a last resort.** Imagine you are in a driverless car, zipping along on the highway, and the AI announces that it needs to do a reboot, right away. This is not the same as doing a reboot on your smartphone when you are playing a video game that froze-up the phone. Developers should consider an on-board reboot as a last resort and only invoked with great caution.

Conclusion

You'll be happy to know that the amount of computer capability packed into a self-driving car is many magnitudes greater than the puny but valiant computers used on the Apollo 11 spacecraft.

Those programmers in 1969 could only dream of someday having access to the incredibly powerful computing that we commonly have available today. Even your smartphone is by far superior in computer power than were the lunar lander computers.

That's though just the hardware side of things.

From a software perspective, we still today can readily have the same kinds of issues occur, and hidden bugs or suddenly appearing faults, which could have happened back in 1969. Let's make sure that we learn the lessons of the past and therefore are extremely mindful when crafting, testing, and fielding autonomous cars.

Thanks goes to NASA and all those involved in getting us to the moon, and hopefully today's driverless cars will be prepared for any 1202 or 1201 codes that might pop-up.

CHAPTER 9

NURO SELF-DRIVING DELIVERY

AND

AI SELF-DRIVING CARS

CHAPTER 9

NURO SELF-DRIVING DELIVERY

AND

AI SELF-DRIVING CARS

How many times have you gotten into your car to simply drive over to a local store to buy an item that you needed at your home?

I'd wager that you've done this at least several times a month, and maybe dozens or more times over the course of a year.

According to USA government statistics published by the Bureau of Transportation Statistics, Americans are making about 1.1 billion car trips per day, overall, and of those journeys nearly 45% of those driving efforts are undertaken for shopping and similar kinds of errands.

That's an astounding number of such relatively routine local trips (around 500 million per day!).

If you multiply it out to an annualized basis, the number comes to around 181 billion car trips per year, merely to get some milk or cookies from the grocery store or go grab that ice maker that you had earlier lent to a friend for their summertime party.

In several of my prior columns, I've analyzed how self-driving driverless cars can be used to undertake the delivery of goods, providing an autonomous driving capability that will tote your groceries to your home, without you having to undertake the driving chore (and nor does anyone else have to do so).

You can merely purchase your desired goods online and your local grocery store could put the vaunted items into a self-driving car, send it on its way to you, and once it has arrived, you grab up your bread, frozen foods, and the like. Then, once you've gotten your items out of the driverless car, the AI would dutifully head the vehicle back to the store, aiming to repeat this cycle over again for other customers.

This notion of undertaking deliveries could be performed by a driverless car, or, for reasons I'll describe in a moment, it might be preferred in some ways to use a vehicle purposely designed for making deliveries that is not a car per se (not a *passenger* car), and instead would be a vehicle specifically made for delivering goods. There are various firms vying vigorously in this niche.

Indeed, last week, I met with Dave Ferguson, co-founder of Nuro, one of the leading firms for developing autonomous delivery vehicles, and we had to chance to chat during the TechCrunch TC Sessions: Mobility summit that took place in San Jose, California on July 10, 2019.

Nuro was launched in 2016 by Dave and his colleague Jiajun Zhu, both of them having previously worked at Waymo on Google's autonomous car initiative. Nuro has racked-up some impressive funding numbers, including having raised in initial rounds approximately $92 million via Greylock Partners and Gaorong Capital, and more recently they received a hefty infusion of $940 million by SoftBank Group, doing so in February of this year.

Let's unpack some of the most notable aspects about autonomous delivery vehicles.

Basis For Aiming At Specialized Delivery Vehicle Versus Using A Car

We'll start by considering the desire to achieve self-driving cars, and then see how we might reshape some of that attention toward self-driving delivery vehicles.

When I gave the keynote speech at last year's AI World conference, I had exhorted that building an autonomous car is a very hard thing to do. Tim Cook, CEO at Apple, has famously said that developing a driverless car is the mother of all AI projects. In spite of some pundits suggesting that self-driving cars are easy to craft and will be roving on our public roadways in droves any day now, the reality is that there is still a long and arduous journey ahead to arrive at such a vision.

During my presentation, I talked about the many attributes associated with a truly autonomous car and pointed out that it is a large-sized multi-headed beast that requires doing a lot on each distinctive portion and then ensuring that all of the myriad of sub-elements are integrated together and work synergistically with each other.

One question that I received from the AI developers in attendance was whether it might be possible to somehow reduce the magnitude of the problem, providing a kind of divide-and-conquer that might solve a significant chunk of the problem, for now, and then allow for a later expansion of the narrowed solution to become eventually a fully robust solution to the overarching problem.

In other words, simplify the problem in some useful and sensible manner, solve it, and keep an eye on being able to ramp-up the simpler solution as feasible.

That's some real-world engineering "problem solving" thinking for you.

My answer was this: *No passengers.*

There was a puzzled reaction to my remark.

What does it mean to reshape the driverless car problem by saying that there can't be any passengers?

If you could excise passengers out of the equation for designing a self-driving car, it would help quite a bit in reducing the overall problem space. I realize you might be pondering what would you do though with a car that cannot hold passengers, and, aha, you could use the resultant driverless vehicle for the delivery of goods (sans any humans inside the vehicle).

Here's what you get by taking out the passenger aspects:

- **Can reduce the size of the vehicle.** Realize that passengers take up a lot of space inside a car, and so if you aren't carrying passengers, you could opt to reduce the interior space, which accordingly would allow you to reduce the overall size of the vehicle, making it smaller than a regular sized car.

- **Reduce the interior complexities.** When you have passengers inside a car, you must have all sorts of safety restraints for them, you need to accommodate their seating needs, etc. Take out the passengers and you can dramatically reduce the interior complexities.

- **No need for AI-to-human inside interaction.** For driverless cars, one of the as yet fully tackled problems will be the Natural Language Processing (NLP) interactions with humans riding in autonomous cars. Right now, this is being treated overly simplistically of just having the rider say where they want to go, but that's not going to be acceptable for when humans are routinely riding in self-driving cars and want to provide guidance such as ad hoc detouring through a fast-food eatery or asking the AI to take them to the nearest emergency room because they are having a medical emergency.

- **Maneuverability options increase.** A driverless car must not make rapid maneuvers that could frighten or harm the human passengers and instead needs to drive in a more muted manner. Without any passengers on-board, the AI has a wider range of maneuvers that it can choose from while using the driving controls.

- **Buffer zone increases.** With a conventional sized car, you need to carefully stay within your lane and have a rather minimal buffer or crumple zone to play with when driving (think about those near scrapes with other cars or having near hits with bike riders). Once you redesign a car to become passenger void, the resulting vehicle can be thinner, which boosts the buffer zone and offers a handy safety margin that you could leverage.

- **Less intrusive.** Passenger-sized cars are unwieldy at times, such as trying to find a parking space large enough to fit your car or doing a double-parking act momentarily since there's no other sizable place to come to a stop. By removing the passenger requirement, and reducing the size of the vehicle, it opens possibilities of places to park or spots for coming to a halt that are a lot easier to find and much less intrusive to other traffic.

- **Reduced impact in incidents.** No matter what some pundits keep saying, we are not going to have zero injuries and nor zero fatalities simply because of having self-driving cars. Inevitably, self-driving cars will have situations that the physics belies any avoidance action and a wayward pedestrian, or a drunken driven car are going to end-up colliding with an autonomous car. In the case of an autonomous delivery vehicle, it is likely that the reduced size and weight would make that impact less harsh than a conventional sized passenger car would.

- **Slower speeds likely.** Humans expect that a self-driving car is going to drive them around in the same manner that human driven cars do, including going at high speeds on freeways, and at times zipping along on highways too. For an autonomous delivery vehicle, you can for now aim to have them go at slower speeds and mainly drive on local streets, rather than using the fast lane approach that human passengers would undoubtedly be insisting upon. For the AI system, being able to go at slower speeds such as the driverless shuttles you see popping up is a lot easier to handle than when at higher speeds.

- **Increased access to more pathways.** You've probably driven a car down an alley and had moments that you worried the car was going to sideswipe parked cars or trash cans. Given the reduced size of a driverless delivery vehicle, it can potentially go places that a car could not readily go, though this obviously needs to be undertaken in a legal and safe manner, meaning that the delivery vehicle cannot just plow along on sidewalks if not so permitted.

I hope you can see that there are a lot of benefits of taking passengers out of the autonomous driving conundrum (I've listed several, there are others that exist too).

Of course, we are a world of people that requires the transport of people, and so don't misinterpret my comments as though I am saying that we don't need driverless cars and only need driverless delivery vehicles. We do need driverless cars.

It would be handy to also have driverless delivery vehicles.

And, if you think of the driverless delivery vehicle as a stepchild of driverless cars, by somewhat constraining the driverless car problem and reshaping it to the no-passengers perspective, you can get a twofer, namely devise and adopt driverless delivery vehicles for their own sake of doing delivery, plus it puts us hopefully a leg-up toward achieving true driverless cars.

How Nuro Is Tackling The Driverless Delivery Vehicle Approach

In my discussion with Dave, we talked about their R1, which is the name they've given to their initial self-driving delivery vehicle model (we joked about the name being rather engineering-like, akin to what you'd expect from engineers thinking about the tech rather than the pizzazz).

At about half the width of a car sedan, the R1 weighs-in at around 1,500 pounds (a conventional midsized cars weighs around 3,000 to 3,500 pounds or so).

Per my comments above, this is an example of how an autonomous delivery vehicle can be thinner than a passenger car, accruing the benefits I've listed, and has less weight as well.

There isn't any passenger designated space in the R1, and instead the interior space is used to carry cargo.

Last year, Nuro got underway with a tryout in conjunction with Kroger, aiming to deliver groceries as the cargo loaded into the R1. In June of this year, Nuro indicated that it is getting into pizza delivery via a relationship with Domino's.

In the autonomous delivery niche, most are designing the vehicle to be exclusively for cargo carrying, while there are some firms toying with the notion that perhaps there should be a place within the vehicle to hold one passenger. The logic is that a store might want to include a human ride-along attendant that would help at the point of delivery (they wouldn't drive the vehicle, just be an aide once the vehicle stops), though this obviously utterly changes the nature of the delivery vehicle since you've now placed back into the equation the needs of having a human passenger.

We'll have to wait and see how the no-passengers versus limited-passenger competing approaches pans out.

Yet another alternative involves having a robot that fits into the cargo space, and upon arriving at the delivery point, the robot climbs out of the vehicle and carries the goods the remaining 10 feet to the door of the customer. The good news about using a robot is that though it technically could be considered a "passenger," I think we all would agree it is really not a passenger per se since it is not a human, and instead you could liken the robot to added "cargo" that just so happens to be able to aid in the overall delivery process.

Conclusion

Dave emphasized that their mission at Nuro is to accelerate the benefits of robotics for everyday life.

In that sense, their self-driving delivery vehicle is one type of robot, on wheels, designed and built to deliver goods, meanwhile their broadly framed mission statement opens other avenues for them to pursue in using various other kinds of robotics systems, down-the-road.

For now, the attention at Nuro is aimed at home deliveries, which certainly is a hefty handful in terms of advancing self-driving tech and exploring how consumers will perceive and accept delivery of their prized pizzas and groceries without a human driver involved.

Plus, the learnings arising from achieving autonomous deliver vehicles can undoubtedly bolster how self-driving cars can advance too.

CHAPTER 10

SAFETY FIRST (SAFAD) APTIV

AND

AI SELF-DRIVING CARS

CHAPTER 10

SAFETY FIRST (SAFAD) APTIV

AND

AI SELF-DRIVING CARS

I recently met with Karl Iagnemma, President of Aptiv Autonomous Mobility and founder of NuTonomy, getting a chance to have a conversation with him about safety in the self-driving cars realm.

We were both at the TechCrunch TC Sessions: Mobility summit in San Jose, California on July 10, 2019, and carved out some riveting moments to collegially chat and engage in an energetic dialogue on the all-important topic of safety of autonomous cars, doing so amongst the rather noisy hubbub and frenetic activity that's a hallmark of these kinds of gatherings.

Dovetailing into our discussion was the recently released white paper entitled "Safety First For Automated Driving," which many are referring to as SaFAD as a handy acronym.

I'll first offer some of my thoughts about the SaFAD and then share with you a curated set of key points that emerged in my in-depth discussion with Karl on the topic of safety and driverless cars.

About The Safety First For Automated Driving Report

The white paper contains an indication of various generic safety aspects about self-driving cars and was jointly put together by 11 companies that are in this burgeoning space.

At around 150 pages of somewhat technical material (though not overly technical, for those that are tech savvy in this niche), another moniker some are colloquially using to refer to the report is "the brick," simply because it is not a typical scant and glossy white paper, and instead covers some quite heavy material and amounted to a relatively longer sized and heftier document.

The companies putting together this report did so collaboratively on a voluntary basis, and there's nothing binding per se about the result, other than it does helpfully start toward a kind of emerging blueprint or template for thinking cohesively and comprehensively about safety of driverless vehicles.

Also, the contents are not specific to any particular automaker or tech firm and covers a myriad of overarching and generic elements underlying the need to include safety principles and practices into the design and deployment of autonomous cars.

The eleven firms that participated in the crafting of the report, as listed in alphabetical order are: Aptiv, Audi, Baidu, BMW, Continental, Daimler, Fiat Chrysler Automobiles, HERE, Infineon, Intel and Volkswagen.

As you can see from the list of firms participating, not everyone in the self-driving car arena happened to get involved in this voluntary effort, though some that did not participate have already come out and said they generally support the resulting white paper.

There are some critics that have expressed qualms that something of this nature is being done outside of the "normal" channels for putting together automotive related standards. As such, they argue that this is interesting and perhaps useful work, but it lacks the kind of official or formal clout that a bona fide standard tends to provide.

In my reading of the paper, it primarily is a bringing together or blending of elements from numerous existing and relevant standards, which the report so acknowledges. In that sense, this particular report is not necessarily breaking new ground and more so an accumulation of other already published formal standards, being put together in a helpful and blended way, perhaps offering a more accessible and readable variant, along with an initial attempt at augmenting it was guiding principles.

For those of you into-the-weeds about autonomous vehicles, here's an indication of the formal standards documents that the white paper acknowledges were used as input to the white paper:

- ISO/PAS 21448:2019 Road Vehicles – Safety of the intended functionality (SOTIF)
- ISO 26262:2018 Road Vehicles – Functional safety
- ISO/SAE CD 21434 Road Vehicles – Cybersecurity engineering
- ISO 19157:2013 Geographic information – Data quality
- ISO/TS 19158:2012 Geographic information – Quality assurance of data supply
- ISO/TS 16949:2009 Quality management systems – Particular requirements for the application of
- ISO 9001:2008 for automotive production and relevant service part organizations
- ISO/IEC 2382-1:1993 Information technology – Vocabulary – Part 1: Fundamental terms
- ISO/IEC/IEEE 15288:2015 Systems and software engineering – System life cycle processes

It's the customary list of related standards, the usual culprits, one might say.

Note that many of those official standards are somewhat piecemeal, covering a particular slant or angle on a narrower topic, while in contrast the SaFAD has attempted to pull together numerous relevant bits-and-pieces from across the spectrum of safety related facets for automated driving. That effort to try and tie together at times disparate standards is contributory in its own right.

The white paper does not try to be something that it is not, fortunately, and right away the document makes it clear that:

"Devising an explicit technical solution or minimum or maximum standard is not included in the scope of
this publication."

"This publication is intended to contribute to current activities working towards the industry-wide
standardization of automated driving."

"The goal of this publication is to provide an overview of and guidance about the generic steps for
developing and validating a safe automated driving system."

I am intentionally pointing out to you those salient boundaries due to the aspect that some in the media have been mischaracterizing the white paper.

I've seen some pundits that have lauded the report as though it is the final word on safety of driverless cars, or that falsely suggest this is a fully comprehensive view, or that intimate that this document will replace existing standards, etc. There are others that are critical of the report as not going far enough and not being deep enough, arguing that to really get to the nitty gritty there would likely need to be (at least) hundreds more pages of added material.

Sadly, in the exuberance of touting the white paper by some and of critiquing it by others, there are those that at times fall into the seemingly ubiquitous "fake news" mania.

Let's call the report what it is, and for which the report authors clearly state what it is. Indeed, here's some additional important scope related matters:

"This is not a one-off publication but should be viewed as a first version."

"The next version should expand the V&V process to include defined solutions with the necessary detail. This could be described via confidence levels and a combination of various testing methods and test results."

"The next version is intended to be put forward as a proposal for international standardization."

There are also some carveouts or exclusions that are explicitly mentioned in the white paper and for which I think that we might all agree are worthy of ultimately getting into any future such document (and bringing into these matters the various standards that exist or are being formulated and are pertinent to the topics at-hand).

For example, here's notable carveouts:

"Due to its focus on safety, this publication does not address topics such as unsupervised machine learning, misuse, data privacy or advanced driver assistance system either."

"Non-safety-relevant elements that are normally part of a customer function, such as a comfortable driving strategy or the fastest navigation from point to point, are also not included in the scope of this publication."

Finally, for those of you especially interested in the topics of Machine Learning (ML) and Deep Learning (DL) for autonomous cars, you might find fruitful the Appendix B of the report, covering Deep Neural Networks (DNN) and the safety challenges arising thereof.

Everyone in the industry that knows about DNN, or what I usually refer to as Artificial Neural Networks (ANN), of which DNN is essentially ANN's of a larger scale, realizes that there's a can of worms associated with trying to test and validate this kind of advanced tech, boding concern since it is being used in a driverless car that is zooming along on a freeway at 70 miles per hour and holds the lives of passengers and others in its neural network "hands" (so to speak).

Overall, here's then a quick recap about the SaFAD report:

- Primarily a blending together of safety related content from existing standards pertaining to self-driving cars, along with added key principles and some other augmented material, offering a handy in-one-place compendium.

- Not fully comprehensive on the topic, nor intended to be, but provides a first shot at piecing together otherwise disparate aspects and fostering a rallying of getting automakers and tech firms in this space to collaborate on safety for driverless cars.

- Has excluded some areas of keen importance and for which will need to be considered in further versions and acknowledges as such.

- It is an encouraging sign of the utility of "coopetition" amongst autonomous car developers and is sorely needed for the advent and emergence of safe self-driving cars.

My Discussion With Karl Iagnemma

Those of you familiar with the self-driving car industry would certainly recognize Karl's name and fame.

In 2013, he founded an autonomous car focused company called NuTonomy, having launched in the "early days" of the soon to arise tsunami of commercial interest in driverless cars. He then sold the company in 2017 to Delphi Automotive PLC, the global auto parts company. There was subsequently a spin-out of some portions of Delphi and then a name change to Aptiv. Karl is President of Aptiv Autonomous Mobility.

During my chat with Karl, we discussed a wide array of topics in the self-driving car realm. I'll cover herein just some of the points, ones that I think offer special noteworthiness.

First, we discussed that it behooves the entire self-driving car industry for the various automakers and tech firms to come together and seek to work collaboratively.

I've previously remarked that the intensity of secrecy and desire to win at achieving the moonshot of getting to a truly autonomous car has often meant that the automakers and tech firms are unwilling to share what they are up to and what could be important for each other. It's hard to blame them for this individualistic practice since there are billions of dollars being poured into these companies and they each need to showcase that they are the "winner" and investments made in them were worthwhile.

I agreed with Karl that it is notable and perhaps even remarkable that these eleven firms were able and willing to work hand-in-hand on the safety matter and put together the white paper.

Of course, as mentioned earlier, there is nothing proprietary contained in the report and so the participating firms did not have to reveal their IP or divulge any inner workings of their systems. In that sense, you could say it was "easier" for them to work together, though it still is an accomplishment, no matter whether there was any inner sanctum stuff involved.

I've remarked that this harks us to the days of "coopetition" whereby firms that are competitors can find common ground to cooperate on.

This brings us to the next notable point.

As Karl and I discussed, the current state of self-driving cars is such that when even one foul incident occurs, involving either a driverless car getting into a crash, there is a corresponding business impact on *all* of the automakers and tech firms devising autonomous cars.

Even though it might be one particular brand and model of self-driving car in one particular place and time that gets mired into an adverse incident, the assumption by the public and others oftentimes is that it is a sign that the world is coming to end for the advent of self-driving cars. This rush to judgement is part of the dual edged sword of self-driving cars, namely that the attention at times is of a miraculous future ahead and driverless cars are the darling of new innovation that will transform our lives, while in the next breath it can be a condemnation of the industry and a swing to the side of asserting that autonomous cars are never going to be.

Thus, the automakers and tech firms involved in this space should be working together, since they will otherwise be considered in one blanket manner anyway, particularly when the road ahead becomes darkened by incidents.

And this brings me to the next notable point.

Those that are expecting perfection in autonomous cars and that there will be zero fatalities and zero incidents are living in a world of fantasy (I've often said that zero fatalities are a zero chance). In the case of a pedestrian that rushes into the street and for which there was insufficient indication of their presence beforehand, the physics of a car is going to mean that the pedestrian can get hit, regardless of whether you had a human driving or an AI system driving.

While chatting with Karl, it came up that the report mentions this similar aspect about the risks associated with self-driving cars:

"Automated driving will improve performance in most situations compared to that of human drivers. However, it will not completely eliminate the risk of accidents or crashes."

If the public-at-large is going to expect that autonomous cars will eliminate all injuries and deaths, there will be a sad reckoning later on.

Now, just so that those safety-minded pundits in the industry don't right away howl, I am not somehow suggesting or implying that if we cannot reach zero that we can therefore just let any amount of risks be undertaken. Nope, not saying that.

In fact, that's why Karl was quite enthusiastic about the report, I believe, since it offers a realistic look at where safety aspects are today and tries to offer a thought-based platform to launch into greater depth on safety for driverless cars, something the report labels as a "positive risk balance."

This brings up the noteworthy point too that there is not one metric alone that can represent safety for self-driving cars. Karl and I discussed that the somewhat defacto measure being used of miles-to-incident is not sufficient and has numerous inherent limitations and downsides (I've written extensively about these metrics, analyzing them carefully).

In short, as a quick recap of the aforementioned major points:

- It's important and vital for the automakers and tech firms to work together collaboratively on how safety should be devised and baked into the autonomous car industry for all (a form of coopetition, one might say).

- Any single adverse incident has the potential for spreading apprehensions across all the automakers and tech firms, regardless of which particular firm was directly involved, and could upset and potentially stall or stop driverless car efforts, thus the firms need to be ready for this and would be better prepared if collaborating accordingly.

- Incidents are going to happen, though this does not mean that the industry should somehow let down its guard, and in fact the industry needs to be doing whatever it can to try and mitigate or prevent incidents, for which SaFAD is one such means.

- There needs to be a balanced framework of what safety means for autonomous cars, going beyond any simple single metric, and be realistic for what our real-world of driving consists of.

Conclusion

Karl and I discussed that it is important for self-driving car firms to be doing a robust combination of scenario-based testing, simulation testing, closed track testing, and on-road testing.

There are some that argue there should not be any public roadway testing until the other methods of testing have "proven" that driverless cars are ready for being on our streets.

The counter-argument involves the notion that with sufficient safety precautions, having on-road testing is worthwhile and necessary, without which it doesn't seem likely that we would see autonomous cars being able to get readied for public roadway efforts (I've examined this in several posted pieces, including taking into account a Linear Non-Threshold or LNT perspective).

Aptiv's Autonomous Mobility entity has been undertaking roadway tryouts in Las Vegas, in conjunction with Lyft, and according to Karl they have performed over 50,000 rides to-date. When the effort there in Las Vegas was first announced, I remember the media attention was nearly over-the-top about it.

Since then, the fanfare has pretty much slimed quite a bit, which, when you think about it, actually is a good sign.

If done well, driverless cars will become part of the everyday fabric of our traffic and not standout per se. That's fine. That's preferred. This is the kind of yeoman effort that will step-by-step, gradually, get us toward self-driving cars. For those expecting overnight success on achieving autonomous cars, put aside that notion, and instead realize that it is going to be a long, incremental approach and safety has to be at top-of-mind for the pace and progress that occurs.

CHAPTER 11

BRAINJACKING NEURALINK

AND

AI SELF-DRIVING CARS

CHAPTER 11

BRAINJACKING NEURALINK

AND

AI SELF-DRIVING CARS

I was speaking at an AI autonomous vehicle industry event this week and was asked whether there is any kind of connection between Elon Musk's efforts with Tesla and his activities with Neuralink, which is his futuristic play on using advanced tech to tap into human brains.

The question was prompted by last Tuesday's Neuralink presentation (on July 16, 2019, see the recorded video here), showcasing Musk and various Neuralink scientists and researchers, touting their newly unveiled wares and software that they've been toiling away on, having crafted it with great intensity and single-minded purposefulness in their souped-up neurotechnology labs.

My answer about the potential connecting tissue between Tesla and Neuralink is that the simplistic answer is there isn't any direct linkage per se (other than Musk himself), but, if you are willing to stretch your imagination, stepping outside most anyone's comfort zone, there might be a synergistic aspect in the realm of self-driving cars.

Yes, I said it, there is a potential connecting perspective via the realm of self-driving cars.

Preposterous, some might retort.

Well, give me a moment to at least explain the logical underpinnings that support such a seemingly outlandish assertion.

Let's start by unpacking what Neuralink is doing.

Unlocking The Human Brain

Neuralink was one of those stealth firms that Musk opted to get underway, doing so in 2016, becoming publicly known later on in 2017, and gained notoriety due to the hiring of several of the world's topmost neuroscientists. You can't really keep a brain trust of this magnitude under wraps for very long (brainiacs about the brain, one might say).

On a practical everyday basis, the stated goal was to be able to better treat brain diseases and that via neurotechnology you could hopefully plant devices into the noggin and overcome or at least mitigate neural disorders.

Like many newborn "hot" tech firms that want to also have a broader vision and see far beyond the near-term trials and tribulations of today's world, they also stated that they were ultimately aiming to enhance humans, essentially bringing to real-life the desires of transhumanism (a philosophy that high-tech should be used to transform humans to a greater plain).

For start-ups that want to swing for the fences, it's crucial to have an out-there kind of aspiration or goal, and undoubtedly Neuralink has one.

Imagine that you could implant electrodes or the equivalent into the human brain.

Suppose further that you could do this without harming the brain, and you could do this without having any visible indication that someone has these in their brain (no protruding antennas, no Frankenstein scars, etc.).

To use the implanted electrodes, there would be a wireless means to communicate with them. Thus, you could have these embedded computer-like elements sitting inside your head, no one else the wiser, and yet you would potentially be the wiser, or maybe at least be better off, as a result of the brain melded apparatus.

This is a really tough problem to solve.

Consider these foundational questions:

- How can you put something into a person's head and yet not kill them or otherwise mar their brain?

- Even if you can get electrodes into the brain, what good will it do if you are unable to detect what is happening inside the brain?

- And, even if you can plant something and even if you can perhaps detect signals of one kind or another, how can you interpret and make sense of those signals such that it relates to what people are actually thinking?

I realize it seems eerie to contemplate putting electronics into someone's head.

You've perhaps seen pictures or videos of various methods and devices being used today, mainly consisting of overly sized, physically intrusive electrodes that stick-out like a porcupine and you can only viably utilize while inside a sterile hospital room or equivalent.

There are some efforts involved in "remotely" detecting the neural signals of the brain by wearing a cap or bowl-like bonnet on your head. These though are oftentimes unable to pinpoint specific neurons and also have to deal with signal degradation and noisiness because of the cranium or skull acting as a kind of ethereal barrier to signal detection.

The initial joke or eye-wink within Neuralink was that Musk wanted them to build a "wizard hat" for the brain.

Zoom forward in time to the Tuesday presentation and you can see that the researchers have gone further than merely aiming at devising a hat.

They have been working on tiny electrodes that can be inserted with the use of tiny threads, doing so with delicate precision as guided by a specially built robotic hand. This also includes an electronic chip that is called the N1 sensor and a wearable device that looks like a petite hearing-aid that you might clip onto your ear (they call it the Link, a portable Bluetooth device that includes a battery).

I'd urge interested readers to look at the Neuralink white paper that describes the particulars of the clever approaches used and shows pictures and diagrams depicting the pioneering devices involved (here's a link to the white paper).

As stated in their white paper, they have been developing a groundbreaking, scalable, high-bandwidth BMI system, encompassing flexible polymer probes, various customized low-power electronics, and can be precisely placed or inserted via the use of an innovative robotic hand. Besides having put together the devices and infrastructure to do this, they have also been running experiments on rats (in accordance with the lab animal guidelines of the National Research Council).

Believe it or not, they have created a smartphone app that you can then use to communicate with the devices inside your head. Instead of watching those endless cat videos, you can watch your brain at work, though it is right now just measuring bio-electrical spikes and signals. Figuring out what those signals signify is still being figured out.

Before you rush to your local store to buy electrodes, please keep in mind that this is an early stage research effort and they have quite a distance to go before this becomes something tangible in terms of life changing for humans.

Also, it might be worthy to note that the brain has an estimated 100 billion neurons (some argue it is closer to 86 billion, which admittedly is nearly 20% less than 100 billion, but anyway, let's not quibble over it). For each neuron, there are biological synapses that are like branches outreaching to other neurons, of which there are an estimated 100 trillion of those.

The Neuralink team suggests that they could potentially insert up to 10,000 electrodes, a huge leap from today's technology, yet if you compare this amazing step-up to the vastness of the brain, you obviously are still relegated to a teeny tiny portion of the universe of neurons in your head.

Musk, always wanting to move faster and make jaw-dropping rapid progress, stated during the presentation that Neuralink might be undertaking real-world trials in a human head, an actual living human patient, before the end of 2020.

He didn't say how to contact them if you want to volunteer, so if you were thinking about it, you'll likely need to wait a bit longer than 2020 to try one out.

Brain Insertion And Self-Driving Cars

In an AI column that I posted nearly two years ago, I had speculated about the progress that we'd see in the field of brain tapping or more properly and formerly referred to as BMI (Brain Machine Interfaces). You might know of this via its slang or streetwise naming, the so-called brainjacking as commonplace vernacular.

It is wonderful to witness the BMI progress being made via the work of Neuralink (absolutely laudable and noteworthy).

With that being said, let's return to my earlier remark that somehow BMI or the capability of tapping into the brain could be leveraged toward the advent of self-driving cars, a likely puzzling comment of intriguing proportions.

I'll start by offering an important utterance by Musk during the Neuralink presentation, whereby he said that the effort to connect with the brain is going to be a type of symbiosis with Artificial Intelligence. He even said that it would be a "go along for the ride" of the brain and AI being able to work together, a virtual merging of a kind, combining what an AI system brings to the table with what the human mind brings to the table.

Couldn't agree more.

The current approach by Neuralink concentrates on being able to detect neural signals in a human's brain and then allow the human to do something about it.

You might for example glance at your smartphone, see that it is displaying the spiking of neurons that have to do with (let's say) being depressed, giving you a handy visual indicator that you are on the verge of a potentially deep and debilitating depression cycle. By having this detection so easily displayed, you might re-focus your mind, aiming to halt the depression in its tracks, doing so before it can grab hold of your brain overall.

Up the ante. If there was a sophisticated AI app on your smartphone, it might be able to interpret those neural signals just as you would have, likely faster, and perhaps alerted you that a depression cycle was festering.

Or, and here's a bit of a controversial next step, the AI might opt to send signals to the electrodes in your head, trying to suppress the depression. This could be done by the AI without having to warn you about the emerging depression. Instead, the AI goes about doing its job, just as though you were using an app to keep you from forgetting where you put your car keys or neglecting to brush your teeth.

Whoa, some say! We have gone from the read-only version of brain tapping and ventured into the write-into the brain variation, a nightmare of sorts to those that doubt the efficacy of such an approach. Couldn't the government then force our minds to be filled with the thoughts that the government alone wanted us to believe? Yes, it opens an ethical can-of-worms, for sure.

That's why the word "brainjacking" is befitting when you are allowing a BMI to cause a change in the neuron signals within the brain. We probably would agree that jacking isn't the right wording if the BMI only was reading from the brain. Once the system is permitted to change the brain by altering signals in neurons, you've entered into an entirely different ballgame and essentially can overtake or jack the mind, presumably, theoretically.

Anyway, I'd like to make this discussion easier by stipulating for the moment that we'll assume the BMI will be read-only (conspiracy theorists won't like the assumption).

Now, let's bring self-driving cars into this picture.

Currently, you drive a car by handling a steering wheel and moving your feet onto and off of an accelerator pedal and a brake pedal. That's the long-time conventional method of manipulating the driving controls.

Some have suggested that with the advent of Siri and Alexa, considered Natural Language Processing (NLP) AI-based systems, maybe humans could merely speak while sitting inside a car and use spoken commands to drive the vehicle. Hey, driving system, please accelerate to 40 miles per hour. Driving system, you are going too fast, slow down to 30 miles per hour. Hey, hits the brakes, hard! And so on.

Not at all practical.

The time it takes to speak such utterances tends to be much lengthier than moving your arms or legs, thus it would be too much of a delay. Your utterances might be misstated, especially when faced with a dire emergency. You also might say the wrong thing, perhaps telling a friend in the car about the time that you hit the brakes, and the voice system mistakenly suddenly jams on the brakes since it assumed you had given it a command. Etc.

What is much faster than voice and even faster than using your arms and legs? Your mind.

Let's suppose you had a BMI device in your head that could connect to your car, doing so wirelessly, just as your smartphone can today connect wirelessly to your car. You get into your car and mentally tell the car to start. It starts. You mentally tell the car to proceed ahead at a pace of 5 miles per hour. The car proceeds ahead.

Before you howl at this seemingly crazy idea, I concede that there are numerous problems or issues with the BMI-to-car approach.

Even if you could master your mental processes to the degree of being able to focus them toward driving the car and doing so in a manner that the BMI can detect, you are undoubtedly skeptical since a person might veer away from the mental effort of driving and suddenly the car has no mental orders being fed to it. Or, maybe the human "driver" is drunk and their thoughts are wild, causing the car to wildly weave across the lanes of the freeway.

Well, remember the symbiosis point.

If the car was AI-equipped, it would be co-sharing the driving with you, and presumably could contend with situations whereby your mind wonders afield or you are in a drunken state-of-mind. Almost like having a sober buddy to help with the driving.

Usually, at this juncture of such a discussion, I have someone say that you might as well have the AI do all of the driving and cutout the human driver. Why deal with the BMI aspects if you don't have to do so, some would argue.

That's the rub.

We don't yet know whether we can get AI to the vaunted Level 5 of being able to fully autonomously drive a car. Some say yes, we can, and others say we aren't going to get there, either for a very long time or possibly never.

As such, if you believe that humans will still need to be involved in the driving task, and that the AI can't make it the "last mile" of being good enough to do so, we might augment the AI with the human brain, using BMI. For example, it's rather apparent right now that we aren't going to crack-the-code anytime soon on human common-sense reasoning, therefore you might allow the AI that doesn't have common-sense reasoning to tap into a human that does have it.

Conclusion

Before you break a gasket and point out that this have lots of unsightly loopholes and guffaws as an approach to driving, I'll just say that I had forewarned you that this is outside-the-box thinking. Maybe outside of the box of the outside-of-the-box thinking.

It's an interesting equation, offering that we might combine BMI with AI, and then combine those with cars, leading us toward either better semi-autonomous cars or fully autonomous ones, though obviously it isn't in the spirit of being truly fully autonomous if the AI is going to be reliant on the human mind for assistance.

There's an argument in there about the notion that suppose your brain was able to interact with the AI of the self-driving car on a subliminal basis, thus, you weren't really taxing your mind per se and it was like you were merely along for the ride (meanwhile your brain was being used to help out).

Does that constitute full autonomy, when you aren't even aware of your brain being so utilized? Most would say that if the mind is used in the tiniest iota, the AI is not truly autonomous.

As relief on this topic, none of this is going to be possible for quite a while, so you can allow your mind to rest easy about this, for the time being.

CHAPTER 12

STORMING AREA 51

AND

AI SELF-DRIVING CARS

CHAPTER 12

STORMING AREA 51

AND

AI SELF-DRIVING CARS

Unless you live in a cave or perhaps are hiding in an underground bunker that lacks internet access, you've likely heard about the Area 51 mania that seems to be sweeping across social media.

In short, a posting on Facebook proposed that people should collectively storm the Area 51 locale, a Nevada military site known for the oft repeated suggestion that maybe aliens from outer space are housed there, and that by spreading the word to make an audacious all-together rush onto the property at the same date it would overwhelm the installation security.

Presumably, as the invite says, the security can't stop them all, and some of the human invaders would finally reach the inner sanctum of Area 51. The posting appears to indicate that so-far a million or more people might want to participate in the forbidden cabal.

The official response to-date by the U.S. military is rather succinct, essentially saying don't do it: "As a matter of practice, we do not discuss specific security measures, but any attempt to illegally access military installations or military training areas is dangerous," says the United States Air Force spokesperson Laura McAndrews.

It is said that the original posting on Facebook was actually intended as a joke. Whether that was the case or not, the matter has blossomed by the accelerated and expansive nature of social media in today's always connected world.

People Of All Mindsets Might Do The Wrong Thing

The people that are clicking that they will attend are composed of a number of likely subcategories.

You've got the ones that are saying they will attend and yet have no intention of attending, likely just wanting to up the hype about the whole thing.

There are the ones that say they are going to attend, and intend to do so, but are coming mainly to watch the others that are presumably going to be there.

And you've got the people that genuinely are aiming to undertake the storming action.

A lousy mixture that will morph during the event, if it happens.

One aspect about mob mentality is how people can change their minds once they enter into an actual mob situation. It could be that people show-up, at first no one trying to storm, and then if they see someone else storm, even just a few nutty ones, it opens a "justification" floodgate and the others decide to follow along.

Then, you'd have the ones that thought they were only coming there to observe that then figure if the others are storming then they will "innocently" follow them, merely to watch what happens (not seemingly realizing they now are also breaking the law, or perhaps betting or hoping that a judge would buy into their classic excuse "I was trying to prevent others from rushing further, your honor").

The whole thing stinks.

The military will undoubtedly have to beef-up security, since otherwise the criticism would be deafening that they took no preventive action. You know that the press and media coverage will be tremendous, acting as another allure for people to show-up. Indeed, it is certainly predictable that some miscreants will come under the hope of getting their one minute of fame, regardless of whether they really care about Area 51 or not, being there for the blaze of attention they can garner.

You can anticipate too that there will be people there trying to push some other agenda, using the Area 51 as a handy backdrop and magnet.

All told, envision in your mind a spread-out desert area that is deserted and not prepared for possibly thousands upon thousands of people.

Traffic snarls galore. People's cars overheat and breakdown. People get hungry and had neglected to bring food. People get stuck there overnight and made no provisions as to where they'll sleep. Medical emergencies arise and yet there is no nearby medical care available. Insufficient bathrooms exist and the sanitary conditions will be very raw.

You get the picture. An ugly picture.

What a perfect storm, if you will. The intersecting of the infamous fame and myths about Area 51, combined with the magnifying effects of social media, offering a "promise" that since not everyone can (statistically) get cuffed, you have some potentially good odds of breaking through.

Whereas on an individual basis you wouldn't be willing to take the chance, hiding in the mob is a risk reducing charm, for many.

Alleged Treasures That Beckon Like A Bright Beacon

Suppose some do actually breakthrough and reach the buildings or other secretive structures on the property, what then.

Well, by gosh, there "must" be hidden treasure there, so the myths foretell.

It's not bundles of cash or piles of gold bars that attract the seekers, and instead the chance to "finally" discover alien creatures that have somehow landed here or been otherwise captured by humans. Anyone that could reach that treasure trove and survive to tell the tale, would seem to have captured the fame flag unlike anyone might have ever achieved before.

With such fame might come glory, riches, and, well, jail time.

I suppose you'd be looking for alien bodies and appendages, akin to what has been popularized in numerous science fiction movies.

No need to though only search for alien creatures, since finding even outer space alien-made goods would be nearly equally compelling. Perhaps an alien flying saucer might be useful to discover. Heck, an alien ray gun or some kind of earth-related alien-crafted breathing apparatus would be huge on its own.

Let's just hope the human scavengers ("stormers") don't accidentally press the wrong buttons and the alien devices suddenly wipe out the entire planet.

Not good.

What Else Might Be There

Believe it or not, there are some that are suggesting that even if there is nothing of an alien space embodiment there, it would still be "worthwhile" to storm the place and find government secrets that have been held back from us all.

Maybe our own government has developed a means to transport people like they do in Star Trek, but the capability is being kept under wraps. Or, perhaps government scientists have devised a cure for all diseases, miraculously, yet have not revealed the cure-all, keeping hidden it for when the world finds itself veering toward a massive onslaught of disease and only "we" will have the right pills to take.

Who knows what might be there, man-made (meaning people or human made), top secret, and a treasure that's obviously not quite as grandstanding as proof of outer space creatures, but still assured of notoriety for the finder of such gems?

During an industry event yesterday that I was speaking at, I was asked whether it might be possible that truly autonomous cars are concealed within Area 51.

Let's unpack that notion.

Autonomous Cars: Existence Or Not

I believe that the questioner was really asking whether or not there might true autonomous cars being kept under wraps by the U.S. military.

We don't yet have any commercial fully autonomous cars, in spite of whatever else you might have heard or read. It doesn't yet exist.

Meanwhile, one can imagine secret AI labs maintained by the U.S. government that are toiling away on developing autonomous cars. Actually, it would be more fitting to say that it is likely autonomous vehicles. There could be autonomous driving jeeps, tanks, troop carriers, and the like.

Furthermore, within autonomous vehicles you can include autonomous submersibles (submarine-like craft that operate autonomously), autonomous surface ships, autonomous drones (you've seen those already, I'm sure), autonomous planes, autonomous rockets, etc.

Focusing on ground-based transport, the question amounts to whether the military might have already achieved a truly autonomous vehicle, perhaps trying it out in the remote desert of Nevada, and not told anyone about it.

This certainly might seem "plausible" as conjecture when you consider that it was the DARPA (Defense Advanced Research Projects Agency) that devised the now-famous autonomous vehicle Grand Challenges in the early 2000's that sparked today's push toward autonomous cars.

For conspiracy theorists, the multiple threads seem to tie together. DARPA aided the launching of autonomous ground vehicles efforts, let's things quiet down, silently watches as commercial efforts start to appear, meanwhile they've been pushing ahead the entire time, having by-now eclipsed everyone and arrived at true autonomous cars and other such transport.

Why not proudly showcase their accomplishment?

The conspiracy mongers would assert that the military is holding back in the same way as the earlier example that I mentioned about the cure-all for diseases. Better to have in your back pocket the ready-to-roll autonomous cars, catching your enemies off-guard.

I'll say this, the government is apparently doing a bang-up job of keeping their truly autonomous cars out-of-sight and not as yet leaked out, if those AI-based vehicles do exist.

The cleverness is quite keen, since there are government labs publicly working on autonomous cars and they often publish in AI and autonomous vehicle journals, along with attending and presenting at AI autonomous vehicle conferences.

Pretty astute ruse to act like they haven't yet cracked the code on achieving truly driverless cars, fooling fellow scientists and engineers, all the while in their hidden backrooms of Area 51 going for joy rides and relishing how they've perfected the technology.

Conclusion

I have no privy knowledge about whether or not the military is sitting upon a horde of fully functioning, fully AI-based, fully capable Level 5 autonomous cars.

I can say that anyone storming Area 51, for whatever reason they might conjure up, please don't do it.

Seriously, the harm, distraction, and utter absurdity of the "proposed" action needs to be condemned.

Of course, the military can likely just turn-on the space alien force field that they confiscated back in 1947 at Roswell, New Mexico. That should repel the stormers.

CHAPTER 13

RIDING INSIDE

AN

AI SELF-DRIVING CAR

CHAPTER 13

RIDING INSIDE

AN

AI SELF-DRIVING CAR

Got into a discussion recently about the mysteries of self-driving cars.

I was on a cross-country flight and the person seated next to me asked me what it is like to be inside a self-driving driverless car, especially once the autonomous car is underway and rolling along on a public roadway.

The question arose after she had noticed that I was doing some work regarding autonomous cars and we traded stories of what we each do for a living.

There definitely appears to be growing interest about what happens within a car that is a self-driving car.

I've been a rider or passenger in numerous different brands and models of driverless cars and done so over quite a number of years, partaking directly in their evolution too, so perhaps I've become somewhat ho-hum and nonchalant about the whole thing.

It would be akin to having flown on airplanes lots of times and eventually you tend to zone-out about the interior of the airplane and the various rituals and activities that typically take place. I recall when my children were very young that they were amazed at flying on planes, and after years of doing so, they today take it in stride as does any frequent flyer.

Of course, airplanes are nowadays a routine and regular way to travel. In spite of the rare instances of plane crashes or untoward incidents, we all tend to consider flying as a relatively low-risk or nearly risk-free way to travel. Sure, when the flight gets bumpy in turbulence, we have a momentary flash of concern, or when we see something odd taking place it gets the hairs up on the back of our necks, but that's generally few and far between occasions while flying these days.

Rare For The General Public To Have Seen One

One of the reasons that people are curious about what it is like to be inside a self-driving car is due to the rarity of actually coming in contact with such a beast.

The overall U.S. population has not had a chance to see a self-driving car with their own eyes, in-person, in spite of the various roadway trials taking place, let alone sit inside one.

The tryouts are in just a select few cities, plus there aren't that many of the driverless cars roaming around. Furthermore, the experimental vehicles are typically being run just during daylight hours. And, they are often kept in the same geofenced area, restricted to certain streets and neighborhoods that the driverless car repeatedly roves around in.

You can usually spot a driverless car by the bulbous equipment placed on the roof of the car, often a racking system that contains sensors, such as LIDAR units.

The older versions of these devices were pretty much bulky and made the car standout right away, you could see one of these bulked-up cars coming from a significant distance away by the comic-looking bulb-like cones on the rooftop. Now, the manner of blending the sensors into the top and throughout the body of the car is increasingly looking streamlined, so much so that you could not only fail to notice a driverless car by its stack of equipment, you could be fooled by a conventional car that has a ski rack or other stuff atop it that would make you guess it might be a self-driving car.

Hint: If you want to impress (fool) your friends and neighbors that you are seemingly using a self-driving car, go ahead and mount a roof rack on your vehicle, place some old audio speakers and any dome-like items on the rack, use black cord or wire that resembles electrical lines, and voila, they will believe you've upgraded to an autonomous car.

Insiders Can Take Test Drives Readily

Those that are involved in the self-driving car industry are often able to go for a drive in the latest versions of autonomous cars by attending industry conferences. Usually, any event focused on autonomous vehicles will have a few automakers or tech firms that are providing tryout rides during the conference.

What's kind of interesting is that the grandiose Consumer Electronics Show (CES) has been providing rides in driverless cars in Vegas each year, undertaken by some of the self-driving car companies that have booths at the annual extravaganza, and yet it seemed like this year the attendees weren't as enamored of going for a ride as they had in the prior years that it was offered.

I have a hypothesis to explain this phenomenon.

The progress of self-driving cars from an outward and even inward perspective of the car has been relatively slow to showcase any visibly new aspects, and therefore if you went in a driverless car last year or the year before, going again would not necessarily present you with any visually dramatic difference.

The differences are generally under-the-hood, so to speak, namely that the AI system and the sensors are getting better at performing the driving chore. That's a harder aspect to witness when you are a passenger in such a vehicle.

In fact, let me disappoint you right now by mentioning that you aren't going to see lots of blinking lights and fancy looking doodads when you get into a driverless car.

Some people assume that the interior must look like the inside of a space capsule, jammed with all kinds of switches, buttons, LED displays, and the rest. Sorry, the inside is rather unimpressive and bland looking, not especially standing out in comparison to any conventional car.

If you go to a closed track or proving ground where they are toying with new advances in various sensors and devices, you would be more likely to see unusual looking electronics either inside or outside and mounted onto the car. Plus, the odds are that there would be an engineer sitting inside the driverless car, typically equipped with a laptop or specialized electronics-reading equipment, and they would be carefully scrutinizing numerous displays.

That's the kind of experience that people assume they will have when getting into a driverless car. Those versions of driverless cars at the closed courses are not ordinarily the ones that are being used on the public roadway efforts. After some new equipment has shown merit at the special track, it will get migrated onto their roadway models and get merged into the mix of on-board systems.

For those of you that have gotten into a driverless shuttle, of which they are gradually being experimentally deployed at airports, hotel areas, retirement communities, and the like, you have a chance to witness self-driving tech.

Though that is generally the case, let's also point out that usually the shuttle is limited to how fast it can go and limited as to where it can go. At times, you probably wouldn't be able to distinguish between a "smart" driverless shuttle in the wild versus a "dumb" shuttle used at a theme park that is confined to a fixed track and has no particular smarts infused into it.

The Imagined Experience

Here's what I believe most people envision when contemplating undertaking a self-driving car experience or journey.

They think about getting into a self-driving car that is going to navigate and traverse public roadways, doing so at human driving speeds, and find its way around everyday obstacles, along with stopping at stop signs, and veering away from bike riders in the street, etc.

All of this being done by an invisible hand, they assume, and for which as a passenger it would be amazing to see that a "ghost" appears to be operating the steering wheel and pedals of the car.

I might need to provide further disappointment, unfortunately, since it is usually the case that a human back-up driver is in the self-driving car with you.

The human back-up driver is supposed to be closely watching the road and be ready in an instant to take the driving controls over. This is a key precautionary and safety aspect that makes sense while the driverless car AI is still an unproven commodity. As such, you might get into a driverless car and be let down to see that a human driver is sitting in the driver's seat.

Say what, you ask, I thought this was a driverless car.

The smiling driver, akin to any driver you might find in a standard Uber or Lyft ridesharing car, will tell you they are there for your safety and you can just pretend that they aren't there.

Because these public roadway tryouts are of keen interest to those that happen to ride in such a car, the human back-up driver is usually trained not only about how to takeover the controls of the car (usually referred to as a "disengagement"), if needed, but they also are trained about how to explain to everyday passengers the magic of the self-driving vehicle.

For those of you that are techies, keep in mind that the back-up driver is unlikely to be a techie, and thus their explanations about the AI systems and sensors will be rather simplistic and rudimentary. Even if you somehow get lucky and the back-up driver is an engineer for the firm, they are usually not allowed to divulge any high-tech secrets and will therefore be quite circumspect in what they say about the self-driving car and its capabilities.

I've seen some passengers become very crestfallen upon scurrying into a self-driving car and then immediately changing their tone and demeanor the moment they realize that the driver's seat won't be empty. Sorry, but it is for your protection and for the protection of any other cars, pedestrians, bike riders, and the like that might get nearby the self-driving vehicle.

As an aside, there are some self-driving cars that have remote accessible driving controls, allowing the human driver to be in the backseat of the self-driving car, or even not inside the car at all, but that's rather uncommon and you'd be unlikely to experience such a setup.

Before I get into additional detail about what its like to be inside a self-driving car while it is on-the-go, I should add some additional points about the risks involved.

Keep in mind that the self-driving car could go awry at any moment. The AI might mistakenly choose to run a red light or fail to avoid an obstacle in the roadway. Assuming there is a human back-up driver inside the self-driving car, you have no guarantee that they will takeover the controls in time to save the vehicle from getting into a car accident.

All in all, you are taking a sizable risk being inside a self-driving car, for now, far beyond the kind of risks that you absorb when you for example get into an airplane.

Of course, if you are at risk while inside the self-driving car, we can logically extend that there is a corpus of risk for those that come near to the self-driving car too. Risk is floating everywhere in the case of self-driving cars, encompassing anyone inside the driverless car and anyone nearby, including drivers in other cars, passengers in other cars, pedestrians walking nearby, motorcyclists coming along, scooter riders, bike riders, and so on.

There are some in the industry that are highly critical of these public roadway tryouts and insist that we should not have self-driving cars on our public roadway at this time. They would say that we are allowing all of us to participate in an experimental venture, whether we are aware of our willingness to do so or not.

The counterargument includes that if the automakers and tech firms only did simulations and closed track efforts, this would either not lead to producing true autonomous cars or would greatly delay their advent. In that sense, if you assume that the sooner driverless cars are readied for public roadway use that the more the lives today being killed or injured in car accidents will be reduced, some argue that it is a necessary balance of taking on risk for the overall good that can come from the existing efforts.

It is a contentious matter.

What Happens In The Inner Sanctum

In any case, let's return to the notion of going for a ride in a driverless car today, doing so on public roadways, and for which you need to be cognizant of the risk that you are taking when you do so, and that even if there is a human back-up driver involved that it does not mean that your risk has gone away.

As earlier stated, the interior of the car is not likely to wow you. Overall, it will seem to be a conventional car.

Another disappointing aspect (sorry!), involves the AI interaction.

In the future, it is envisioned that an AI system will dialogue with you, akin to how Alexa or Siri does today, and be able to discuss with you where you want to go, along with possibly offering suggestions about the driving journey that will take place. This use of Natural Language Processing (NLP) and socio-behavioral elements pertaining to the driving act and passenger interactions does not yet exist in any robust manner.

Today, you can anticipate that the human back-up driver will interact with you rather than the AI system, plus you might be able to use a crude mobile app to convey to the driverless car some simple aspects such as the street address or location that is your desired destination.

I often characterize the first-time experience of going for a ride in a driverless car as consisting of several distinct stages or phases that the passenger will undergo. You might be familiar with say the stages of life or the stages of grief that psychologists describe when someone suffers the loss of a loved one.

I've come up with the "eight stages" for first-time driverless car riders:

1. Excitement
2. Trepidation
3. Awe
4. Questioning
5. Realization
6. Complacency
7. Cautionary
8. Realignment

Here's the scoop on the eight stages.

Upon first entering into the driverless car, you'll be excited about the prospects of not only going for a ride with a machine at the wheel (kind of), but also experiencing something historic. Presumably, years from now, driverless cars will be ubiquitous. They will be considered mundane and nothing to write home about.

Meanwhile, you'll be able to tell those that will listen that long ago, you got a ride in a driverless car, before there were driverless cars.

As earlier alluded to, after settling into the self-driving car, you will realize that there is (likely) a human back-up driver sitting there in the driver's seat. You'll still be able to see the steering wheel moving on its own, most of the time, perhaps all of the time, yet admittedly having a person there takes the air somewhat out of the excitement.

Once the driverless car starts on the journey, you are bound to have some moments of trepidation.

Today's AI driving systems are not usually as adept at driving a car as a human would during the even routine aspects of driving. You'll realize that the car appears to be taking extraordinary precautions, often coming to a full stop at stop signs, the kind of full stop that you actually come to a complete halt, wait a moment or two, and then proceed.

This is in contrast the human used rolling-stop that most of us see and do all the time.

The trepidation shifts into awe, once you decide that it seems like the car is doing an adequate job of driving, akin to a novice that is unsure about being on the roadways and often is skittish at the wheel.

You'll at this juncture have lots of questions about what the AI can and cannot do as part of the driving task. The human back-up driver can usually answer those questions, at least at a high-level.

You'll then adjust your earlier expectations and have a realization of what today's self-driving cars can actually do. This is followed often by a sense of complacency. You are sitting in a car and it is taking you to where you want to go. Assuming that nothing untoward happens, the journey gets boring.

If there are any hiccups or close calls during the trip, you'll shift into a cautionary mindset.

Finally, assuming the trip goes without incident, you'll get out of the driverless car at your destination and realign your thinking. It wasn't a knock-your-socks off kind of experience. No sensational or dire aspects (hopefully).

Conclusion

For first timers, if you ask them afterward whether they'd go for a ride in a driverless car again, usually their answer is "it depends."

Anyone in a rush to get to their destination is unlikely to clamor for a driverless car for their riding trip, since the AI systems are currently programmed to be extremely cautious. Also, without an interacting AI voice system, and with the human back-up driver present, the ride is nothing seemingly extraordinary or astonishing per se.

If you have all the time in the world, and you want to brag about your trip, you'd aim to go again.

That's what it is like to go for a ride in a self-driving car of today.

CHAPTER 14

ACES ACRONYM

AND

AI SELF-DRIVING CARS

CHAPTER 14

ACES ACRONYM

AND

AI SELF-DRIVING CARS

It seems like acronyms abound in all fields of endeavor, and sometimes remain arcane and known only to specialists in that domain, but occasionally manage to breakout of their bubble and become widely used and accepted (notable examples would be MRI and EKG, originally used by medical experts and eventually commonly uttered).

Here's an acronym in the self-driving driverless cars niche that you ought to know, namely "ACES" which variously stands for Autonomous, Connected, Electric, and Shared. Memorize it. Put it into your vocabulary. Start using it. Expect to see it, a lot.

It is emerging as the megatrend potent combination, converging together the four biggest disruptions altering mobility and transportation, and arguably a signpost of a transformative wave impacting all of society.

What ACES Means For You

Each of the letters of the ACES acronym are indicative of a megatrend in of itself, so let's consider what each word or phrase means.

Autonomous

Autonomous refers to the advent of autonomous vehicles, especially self-driving driverless cars. The current crop of such cars are primarily semi-autonomous, generally requiring that a human driver be present and ready to co-share the driving task. Getting to the vaunted Level 5, a true driverless car requiring no human driving interventions, offers the hope for vastly enhancing our mobility. You can command your true driverless car at any time of the day, any day of the week, using it to transport you, or run an errand, and you don't need to drive it and you don't need to get someone to drive it for you.

Connected

Connected refers to the electronic connectedness or connecting of cars, allowing cars to both send out and receive electronic messages and information. There is V2V (vehicle-to-vehicle) electronic communications, along with V2I (vehicle-to-infrastructure) that connects vehicles and the roadway system such as traffic lights indicating red or bridges saying they are closed, and V2P (vehicle-to-pedestrians) allowing cars and those pesky pedestrians to electronically alert each other. It is easiest to refer to all of those V's as V2X, wherein X is a variable and you can plug-in any letter you like. There is also OTA, Over-The-Air, which refers to being able to download data and software updates into a car from the cloud, along with uploading data from a car into the cloud.

Electric

Electric refers to the electrification of vehicles, or simply stated the emergence of Electric Vehicles (EV). Just the letter E is used in ACES, otherwise you'd have ACEVS if you jammed the "EV" into the acronym, which does not roll-off the tongue easily. Besides the obvious ecological reasons used to support the advent of EV's, in the case of autonomous cars there is a particular benefit of using an EV, namely the driverless car's craving for electrical power (due to the abundance of sensors and processors). Using an EV is ready-made for electrically fueling the autonomous capability.

Shared

Shared refers to the likelihood that the shift toward ridesharing will continue to grow. Studies suggest that the Gen Z and latest generations are tending away from owning cars and prefer instead to ride in a car that's driven for them. Right now, the ridesharing driving is mainly human based. But how many humans will want to perform ridesharing and might there be a limit that will reduce supply, thus increase the cost to get human drivers, and begin to shove ridesharing (already a loss leader) into worsened shape? Presumably, autonomous cars will solve that dilemma.

It's A Synergistic Heaven

That's a quick explanation of the ACES elements. Each stand on its own, meaning that you can expect them individually and distinctly to progress and alter our world. In addition, there is a synergy that magnetically is drawing them together, each feeding off of the other.

Here's how that works.

Autonomous leverages connectedness to boost what a driverless car can do, communicating with other cars and the roadway and pedestrians, which then is powered by the electric prowess and battery of the self-driving car, which enables ridesharing by taking the human driver out of the vehicle. Ridesharing becomes more viable. That's how these seemingly siloed areas have come together as a fruitful amalgamation.

More Names Than You Can Count

The ACES acronym is not alone.

Some prefer to use CASE (Connected, Autonomous, Shared, Electric) as the acronym, but I think the ACES is catchier and likely to prevail. There is a contingent that insists on SAEV (Shared, Autonomous, Electric Vehicles), but this omits connectedness, plus it is a somewhat unpronounceable moniker.

The automotive industry already has a standard known as Aftermarket Catalog Exchange Standard, which is another ACES acronym, but I think that the broader ACES will overtake this rather narrower version of such a handy ACES signature. Then there is NASA's Advanced Control Evolvable System, another ACES, and there is a driverless car industry verbiage about wanting to have an Autonomous Connected Efficient Safe (ACES) car.

The multitude of ACES makes sense because it is a catchy way to describe something, rather than an oddball collection of letters that no one can remember or speak aloud intelligently.

Conclusion

I believe that the "real" ACES, Autonomous, Connected, Electric, Shared, will increasingly be used and ultimately proclaimed as the proper way to refer to the megatrend's conjunction underway.

You've now learned the secret password that gets you into the dialogue about what the mobility future holds. No need to hide the password, instead you are welcome to use it, impressing friends and colleagues, along with perhaps helping to propel the advent of ACES for us all.

Secret revealed and you don't need to feel guilty about leaking it to others.

CHAPTER 15

KIDS BIKE RIDING

AND

AI SELF-DRIVING CARS

CHAPTER 15

KIDS BIKE RIDING

AND

AI SELF-DRIVING CARS

A recent study reported that kids in the United States are no longer riding their bikes as much as they used to do, and the annual numbers continue to aim downward, slipping further and further into less and less bike riding.

Besides this being a bad sign for the bike makers, especially since bike riding tends to be acquired when young and then carried over into adulthood (thus, the pipeline is thinning), the other concern is that the lack of bike riding is not being replaced by some other equal or better physical activity. It would be one thing if kids opted to say go running or jogging or used the bike riding time to play a sport, but it appears that the bike riding time is giving over to (in essence) motionless sitting.

By motionless sitting, I mean that some claim that the youth of America are using their bike riding time to instead play online video games. Though playing a video game can exert some energy and spirit, most would concede that it is not the physical equivalent of the health benefits from riding a bike.

Video game playing is a more so sedentary task, and beyond building up perhaps stronger finger muscles to manipulate the game controls, it seems doubtful that your child will have generated impressive ripped abs or tiger muscles after hours of Fortnite playing.

Apparently, the volume of kids regularly riding their bikes has decreased by about a million such children over the last four years. Sales of children's bikes dropped by 7.5% in quantities sold over the last year. Regular biking is considered taking rides around your neighborhood, riding to the park or events, and also encompassed the heads-down competitive bike riding realm too. Per national stats, bike riding tends to be done in urban areas (71%), and slightly more so in daylight (51%) than in darkness.

Health and fitness proponents, along with bike makers and retailers, say that this disturbing trend of less bike riding should be a banner alerting us that that something needs to be done to get more kids on bikes. The idea is twofold, more kids riding bikes, plus kids riding their bikes more often.

I'd like to offer a modest proposal about why kids aren't riding their bikes as much, along with a proposed solution that might be coming down the pike, namely, it has to do with human drivers as the problem and self-driving driverless cars as the solution.

Hear me out on this.

Scary To Ride A Bike In Today's Driver Unfriendly Environment

When my children started riding their bikes, I realized that there was a big difference between riding bikes when I was a child and the current environment of riding on today's traffic clogged and traffic endangering streets.

The significant difference that I observed was the emergent wildness of human drivers in their cars, most of whom seem to no longer care much about bike riders, perhaps even more so kids on bikes (children are often lower profile than adults, can be harder to see or predict in terms of movement, and are less aware of being mindful of cars and wayward car drivers).

In an earlier era, it seemed that car drivers were conscientious about watching for and avoiding bicycle riders. Nowadays, just as drivers won't pull over when they hear a siren or see an oncoming ambulance that is flashing its lights, it seems that the mainstay of drivers is also giving short shrift to bike riders.

In a bit of irony, or perhaps just plain infuriatingly, the growth of bike lanes does not seem to have prodded drivers to be more cautious about bike riders.

On a daily basis, I see drivers that weave into bike lanes. I see cars that decide to park in a bike lane, apparently because it is easy to do so, since naturally the bike lane is otherwise free of any obstructions (duh!). All in all, it appears by informal observation that bike riders aren't getting insufficient attention by car drivers. It is as though the painted line that demarks the bike lane is invisible, or maybe the line is an attractor for some drivers, but in any case, a marking on the street is not enough of a barrier to prevent a multi-ton car from being steered into the path of a bike rider, sadly so.

Going beyond my intuition, consider the statistics reported by the Center for Disease Control (CDC), which tracks and reports on bike related injuries and deaths.

The CDC's latest available numbers are that about 1,000 bicyclists are killed each year in the U.S., and around 467,000 bicyclists are injured. Besides the human toll, the CDC also estimates that the dollar cost to our society is approximately $10 billion dollars as a result of medical expenditures and lost productivity in the aftermath of a biking incident.

I realize that you might be saying right now that you are a very safe driver and would never cut-off or barge into a bike rider. In fact, you might even be voicing a complaint that bike riders often are impolite, out-of-control, and do not abide by the rules of the road.

Let me make clear that I am not saying that all drivers are bike seeking monsters, and nor am I suggesting that all bike riders are blameless in terms of getting themselves into hot water. The world of bike riding is a two-way street, metaphorically meaning that the bike riders need to do their part in riding safely, just as the human drivers need to do so too.

In any case, I noticed that my children and their friends all realized the dangers of bike riding in today's world, and it contributed, I believe, toward their hesitancy to go bike riding. Yes, even young kids can be that sensible.

How much did the push away from bike riding due to the fear of crazed car drivers add to the pull of spending time instead on playing video games? I can't pin it down per se, though I think it is fair to assert that if bike riding was able to be done with much less looking over the shoulder, I'm pretty sure there would be a lot more biking riding going on.

Self-Driving Cars Might Be A Spur Toward Bike Riding

Let's assume for a moment that we will ultimately have self-driving driverless cars.

I'm referring to autonomous cars, ones that have the AI system doing the driving and there is no human driving involved. Most of today's modern cars require co-sharing of the driving task between the automation and a licensed human driver, considered Level 2 and Level 3 cars, while the hope is to eventually get to Level 4 and Level 5 as fully autonomous cars.

In theory, a properly developed, tested, and fielded autonomous car will be as safe or presumably safer than human drivers. When it comes to respecting bike lanes, overall it would seem likely that the AI system would be more adherent to staying out of the bike lanes, and also be more attentive to the actions of bike riders.

As such, the increase in roadway safety might lure bike riders back onto the streets, including kids that could be newly introduced to bike riding that otherwise hadn't tried it, and also for children that started bike riding but gave up in concern for getting injured or killed.

I know that some view this idea with either skepticism or argue that the point is actually counterintuitive.

If we really do end-up with self-driving cars, and those vehicles are readily prevalent, and they are relatively low in cost to use for ridesharing or ride-hailing purposes, it would lead one to assume that people, including kids, will ride bikes even less so than now, and will be using cars more so than now. Parents won't need to drive their kids to school anymore since the autonomous car will take on that duty. Thus, the allure and ease of using a car will be so inviting that it will ruin any remaining impetus to go bike riding.

Well, yes, that could happen.

I'm going to use the glass-is-half-full viewpoint and claim that the enhanced roadway safety will spark parents and kids to revisit bike riding. Furthermore, the added convenience of sitting in a car to get someplace will be an instigator for parents to get their kids to do some kind of physical activity, including bike riding.

On top of that, the kids desire to use online video games might be somewhat satiated (if that's possible) by being able to play while inside the driverless car, which will readily have fast internet access such as 5G. This could shift the time devoted to video game playing from the time periods when kids today are at-home play online games to instead use some of that time for bike riding, regularly.

It could be the saving grace for a rejuvenation of getting more kids bike riding and more of the time.

Conclusion

Which do you think we'll see:

- A continued downward spiral of kids not going bike riding, and for which this will hit rock bottom once the advent of self-driving cars arises (that's the pessimistic view), or

- Do you think (perhaps optimistically) that the driverless car emergence will make our roads safer for bike riders and encourage kids to get outside and ride their bikes.

Though it's a guess on my part, I'm going to keep my bikes in good shape and ready for a future when bike riding becomes a grand everyday activity, once again, fueled in some ways by the autonomous cars that will be cruising our roadways.

CHAPTER 16

LIDAR NOT DOOMED

AND

AI SELF-DRIVING CARS

CHAPTER 16

LIDAR NOT DOOMED

AND

AI SELF-DRIVING CARS

I think it is safe to say that most of us would prefer to not be doomed. Suppose someone pointedly tells you that you are doomed in your career or that you are doomed to not get your college degree, or maybe that you are doomed to get mauled by a bear during your next camping trip. Ouch, these are all quite rough prophecies. Is the person making such assertions being perhaps overly malicious, fallacious, outrageous, helpful, insightful, hurtful, or what?

Maybe the doomsayer has got their finger on the pulse of what is taking place and can truly anticipate what the future will bring. Or, it could be that the doomster has other motives for making their proclamations. One approach to assessing the doomsday predictions involves examining the doomsayer to understand what prompts their claims, but this sometimes falls into a bit of an ad hominem kind of debate (focusing on the character of the predictor, more so than the basis for the prediction).

A sound approach involves carefully and logically trying to ferret out whether the doom-and-gloom has any sensible basis underlying it.

As readers of my column might recall, I had previously covered the Tesla Investor Autonomy Day event that involved Elon Musk making various announcements about what Tesla is seemingly going to do, along with his unequivocally brash predictions about what will happen to others trying to make autonomous cars.

Here's what he defiantly proclaimed about other autonomous car makers: "LIDAR is a fool's errand. Anyone relying on LIDAR is doomed. Doomed!"

Nearly all of the autonomous car makers are making use of LIDAR, other than Tesla. Thus, Musk's comments were pretty much a blanket statement slurring just about everyone else in the autonomous car niche. That's some gutsy effrontery.

What's the doom? In other words, where's the meat?

I'll walk you through the presumed logic about why they are all seemingly "doomed" and once I've done so, I believe that it will be relatively apparent that the doomsday prediction is plainly specious.

Background About LIDAR

For quick background, LIDAR is a mash-up of light and radar, a type of sensory device that can be used for driverless cars.

You've likely seen pictures or videos of those bulbous-looking devices on the top of a self-driving car, which it turns out is a LIDAR device being used to aid the AI during the driving task. Essentially, the sensor sends out light beams, the beams bounce off objects, the returning beams are sensed by the LIDAR, and out of this it is possible to try and construct a kind of 3D model of what surrounds the driverless car.

Plus, there is a burgeoning marketplace of LIDAR makers, including some that have been in the industry for years, and others that are eagerly trying to get into the industry.

There is a rapid effort by the LIDAR makers to significantly enhance LIDAR, including having less costly hardware, smaller sized hardware that is less intrusive looking, adding tech related advances to further the LIDAR detection capabilities, and bolstering the software needed to deeply analyze and interpret the captured data.

As per Musk's comments, it seems that he believes that they are all doomed.

Yikes, this suggests that all those other autonomous car makers are somehow marching along a dead-end path, and that all those LIDAR makers and all of the VC/PE investments toward LIDAR are pouring money into a losing proposition. This would be a quite unsettling doomsday end, sad and indisputably undermining the emergence of autonomous cars, if somehow it were the case.

Ways In Which Doom Might Occur

I'd like to address each of the seemingly evocative ways in which an autonomous car maker might be doomed as a result of using LIDAR. For any of the automakers or tech firms that are wondering whether they might be doomed by using LIDAR, perhaps this will be an instructive indication about where such doom or ruination might somehow lurk, if at all.

Implied Claim #1: Doom by using only LIDAR and nothing else.

If an autonomous car maker were to use only LIDAR and not use anything else, such as foregoing the use of cameras and vision processing, I would certainly say that the autonomous car is most likely to be doomed, since there would not be an appropriate balance of multiple sensory means to gauge the world around the driverless car.

But, let's be clear, I've not seen or heard of any autonomous car maker that has taken the (absurd) stance that they are only going to use LIDAR and nothing else. I'm ready to declare any such autonomous car maker as a dolt if they tried this.

Reject this claim as specious.

Implied Claim #2: Doom because somehow LIDAR won't work.

LIDAR is already being used in most of today's driverless cars. In fact, a recent study took camera captured data and recast it into a pseudo-LIDAR data transform, partially showcasing that the algorithms used for LIDAR can improve the capability of analyzing visual data and vision processing. Furthermore, there is ongoing and tremendous amount of research being done to do even more with LIDAR data and capabilities.

Need to reject this claim as specious.

Implied Claim #3: Doom as a result of preoccupation with LIDAR over other sensors such as cameras.

It would seem that Musk is perhaps especially pitching the notion that LIDAR will be a type of crutch (which he's so stated), suggesting that autonomous car makers will be preoccupied by LIDAR to the detriment of giving proper due to cameras and other sensors beyond LIDAR.

This presumes that those other autonomous car makers are (once again) seemingly dolts. It is well-known in the field of autonomous cars that there needs to be a balance of the myriad of sensory methods and that it is essential to strive toward having the best possible sensory capabilities in all respects. Anyone that shortchanges any one sensory approach is gearing themselves up for a lopsided sensor fusion and a kind of blindsiding by not being able to robustly discern the environment around the driverless car.

One supposes that it could happen that an autonomous car maker might undercut their cameras, but I've not seen and nor heard of any bona fide autonomous car maker that has allowed themselves to sacrifice on the camera side to boost their LIDAR use.

Rejecting this claim as specious, but the warning aspect is dutifully noted.

Implied Claim #4: LIDAR might be overly complex to utilize

LIDAR is a relatively complex kind of sensory device and perhaps less simple in comparison to say cameras or conventional radar. It's not clear though that having complexity in of itself is a warranted basis for somehow rejecting a technology, since indeed there are often quite complex devices that provide extremely advantageous capabilities.

Any autonomous car maker that goes into adopting LIDAR is presumably going to ensure that they have the right kind of expertise to leverage LIDAR. I would say that any driverless car maker that unprofessionally shoves LIDAR into place and has no expertise in what they are doing, well, once again they'd make my dolts list. Further, if anyone did somehow skirt around properly applying LIDAR, I think it would become readily apparent right away as to their autonomous car being unable to sufficiently undertake the driving task.

Got to reject this claim as specious.

Implied Claim #5: LIDAR is alleged as overly costly and overly bulky

If I told you that I have for you a mobile phone that weighs about 20 pounds and costs $4,000, what would you say?

I think you would assume that I had lost my marbles.

Well, in 1982, that's what the first commercial mobile phones weighed and costed. You would likely rebuff my offer because you know that in today's world the size of mobile phone is much less, and the costs are much less than they once were.

The claims about LIDAR being overly costly and overly bulky were true at an earlier time of LIDAR evolution but living in the past doesn't make much sense now, and the newest version of LIDAR units continue to come down in price and size.

Specious claim.

Conclusion

Herein, I've tried to ferret out why there might be a basis, a logical and rationale basis, for trying to claim that those using LIDAR for autonomous cars are doomed.

The only means to get there seems to be if the autonomous car makers doing so are dolts. Given the vast amount of attention and dollars going toward these autonomous car efforts, it seems a bit over-the-top to label them all as dolts, presumably lemmings that cannot see past their own failings, and plaster them all as being blissfully unaware of their pending ruin, seemingly due to a head-in-the-sand misuse or misapplication of LIDAR.

The doomsayer might believe that everyone else will be dolts, especially when taking a contrarian view and opting to not use LIDAR. There could be a bit of ego added into the equation by the anti-LIDAR proclaimers, fueled by other successes and a belief in self-empowerment. Some point out that it behooves the anti-LIDAR camp to take pokes at the LIDAR adopters, justifying their posture of opposing the use of LIDAR, along with the aim to save face when confronted about not using LIDAR.

Anyway, let's keep a keen watchful eye on those using LIDAR and ascertain whether they are ill-fated, but this also brings up that what's good for the goose is good for the gander, namely let's also watch those that are anti-LIDAR and see how they fare.

APPENDIX

APPENDIX A

TEACHING WITH THIS MATERIAL

The material in this book can be readily used either as a supplemental to other content for a class, or it can also be used as a core set of textbook material for a specialized class. Classes where this material is most likely used include any classes at the college or university level that want to augment the class by offering thought provoking and educational essays about AI and self-driving cars.

In particular, here are some aspects for class use:

o   <u>Computer Science</u>. Studying AI, autonomous vehicles, etc.

o   <u>Business</u>. Exploring technology and it adoption for business.

o   <u>Sociology</u>. Sociological views on the adoption and advancement of technology.

Specialized classes at the undergraduate and graduate level can also make use of this material.

For each chapter, consider whether you think the chapter provides material relevant to your course topic. There is plenty of opportunity to get the students thinking about the topic and force them to decide whether they agree or disagree with the points offered and positions taken. I would also encourage you to have the students do additional research beyond the chapter material presented (I provide next some suggested assignments they can do).

RESEARCH ASSIGNMENTS ON THESE TOPICS

Your students can find background material on these topics, doing so in various business and technical publications. I list below the top ranked AI related journals. For business publications, I would suggest the usual culprits such as the Harvard Business Review, Forbes, Fortune, WSJ, and the like.

Here are some suggestions of homework or projects that you could assign to students:

a) Assignment for foundational AI research topic: Research and prepare a paper and a presentation on a specific aspect of Deep AI, Machine Learning, ANN, etc. The paper should cite at least 3 reputable sources. Compare and contrast to what has been stated in this book.

b) Assignment for the Self-Driving Car topic: Research and prepare a paper and Self-Driving Cars. Cite at least 3 reputable sources and analyze the characterizations. Compare and contrast to what has been stated in this book.

c) Assignment for a Business topic: Research and prepare a paper and a presentation on businesses and advanced technology. What is hot, and what is not? Cite at least 3 reputable sources. Compare and contrast to the depictions in this book.

d) Assignment to do a Startup: Have the students prepare a paper about how they might startup a business in this realm. They must submit a sound Business Plan for the startup. They could also be asked to present their Business Plan and so should also have a presentation deck to coincide with it.

You can certainly adjust the aforementioned assignments to fit to your particular needs and the class structure. You'll notice that I ask for 3 reputable cited sources for the paper writing based assignments. I usually steer students toward "reputable" publications, since otherwise they will cite some oddball source that has no credentials other than that they happened to write something and post it onto the Internet. You can define "reputable" in whatever way you prefer, for example some faculty think Wikipedia is not reputable while others believe it is reputable and allow students to cite it.

The reason that I usually ask for at least 3 citations is that if the student only does one or two citations they usually settle on whatever they happened to find the fastest. By requiring three citations, it usually seems to force them to look around, explore, and end-up probably finding five or more, and then whittling it down to 3 that they will actually use.

I have not specified the length of their papers, and leave that to you to tell the students what you prefer. For each of those assignments, you could end-up with a short one to two pager, or you could do a dissertation length paper. Base the length on whatever best fits for your class, and the credit amount of the assignment within the context of the other grading metrics you'll be using for the class.

I mention in the assignments that they are to do a paper and prepare a presentation. I usually try to get students to present their work. This is a good practice for what they will do in the business world. Most of the time, they will be required to prepare an analysis and present it. If you don't have the class time or inclination to have the students present, then you can of course cut out the aspect of them putting together a presentation.

If you want to point students toward highly ranked journals in AI, here's a list of the top journals as reported by *various citation counts sources* (this list changes year to year):

- o Communications of the ACM
- o Artificial Intelligence
- o Cognitive Science
- o IEEE Transactions on Pattern Analysis and Machine Intelligence
- o Foundations and Trends in Machine Learning
- o Journal of Memory and Language
- o Cognitive Psychology
- o Neural Networks
- o IEEE Transactions on Neural Networks and Learning Systems
- o IEEE Intelligent Systems
- o Knowledge-based Systems

GUIDE TO USING THE CHAPTERS

For each of the chapters, I provide next some various ways to use the chapter material. You can assign the tasks as individual homework assignments, or the tasks can be used with team projects for the class. You can easily layout a series of assignments, such as indicating that the students are to do item "a" below for say Chapter 1, then "b" for the next chapter of the book, and so on.

a) What is the main point of the chapter and describe in your own words the significance of the topic,

b) Identify at least two aspects in the chapter that you agree with, and support your concurrence by providing at least one other outside researched item as support; make sure to explain your basis for disagreeing with the aspects,

c) Identify at least two aspects in the chapter that you disagree with, and support your disagreement by providing at least one other outside researched item as support; make sure to explain your basis for disagreeing with the aspects,

d) Find an aspect that was not covered in the chapter, doing so by conducting outside research, and then explain how that aspect ties into the chapter and what significance it brings to the topic,

e) Interview a specialist in industry about the topic of the chapter, collect from them their thoughts and opinions, and readdress the chapter by citing your source and how they compared and contrasted to the material,

f) Interview a relevant academic professor or researcher in a college or university about the topic of the chapter, collect from them their thoughts and opinions, and readdress the chapter by citing your source and how they compared and contrasted to the material,

g) Try to update a chapter by finding out the latest on the topic, and ascertain whether the issue or topic has now been solved or whether it is still being addressed, explain what you come up with.

The above are all ways in which you can get the students of your class involved in considering the material of a given chapter. You could mix things up by having one of those above assignments per each week, covering the chapters over the course of the semester or quarter.

As a reminder, here are the chapters of the book and you can select whichever chapters you find most valued for your particular class:

Companion Book By This Author

Advances in AI and Autonomous Vehicles: Cybernetic Self-Driving Cars

*Practical Advances in Artificial Intelligence (AI)
and Machine Learning*

by

Dr. Lance B. Eliot, MBA, PhD

This title is available via Amazon and other book sellers

Companion Book By This Author

Self-Driving Cars:
"The Mother of All AI Projects"

by Dr. Lance B. Eliot, MBA, PhD

This title is available via Amazon and other book sellers

Companion Book By This Author

Innovation and Thought Leadership on Self-Driving Driverless Cars

by Dr. Lance B. Eliot, MBA, PhD

This title is available via Amazon and other book sellers

<u>Companion Book By This Author</u>

New Advances in AI Autonomous Driverless Cars Self-Driving Cars

by Dr. Lance B. Eliot, MBA, PhD

<u>Chapter Title</u>

This title is available via Amazon and other book sellers

Companion Book By This Author
Introduction to
Driverless Self-Driving Cars
by Dr. Lance B. Eliot, MBA, PhD

This title is available via Amazon and other book sellers

Companion Book By This Author

Autonomous Vehicle Driverless Self-Driving Cars and Artificial Intelligence

by Dr. Lance B. Eliot, MBA, PhD

This title is available via Amazon and other book sellers

Companion Book By This Author

Transformative Artificial Intelligence Driverless Self-Driving Cars

by Dr. Lance B. Eliot, MBA, PhD

This title is available via Amazon and other book sellers

Companion Book By This Author

Disruptive Artificial Intelligence and Driverless Self-Driving Cars

by Dr. Lance B. Eliot, MBA, PhD

<u>Chapter Title</u>

This title is available via Amazon and other book sellers

Companion Book By This Author

State-of-the-Art
AI Driverless Self-Driving Cars

by Dr. Lance B. Eliot, MBA, PhD

Chapter Title

This title is available via Amazon and other book sellers

Companion Book By This Author

Top Trends in
AI Self-Driving Cars

by Dr. Lance B. Eliot, MBA, PhD

Chapter Title

This title is available via Amazon and other book sellers

Companion Book By This Author

AI Innovations and Self-Driving Cars

by Dr. Lance B. Eliot, MBA, PhD

Chapter Title

This title is available via Amazon and other book sellers

Companion Book By This Author

Crucial Advances for
AI Self-Driving Cars

by Dr. Lance B. Eliot, MBA, PhD

This title is available via Amazon and other book sellers

This title is available via Amazon and other book sellers

Pioneering Advances for AI Driverless Cars

by Dr. Lance B. Eliot, MBA, PhD

<u>Chapter Title</u>

This title is available via Amazon and other book sellers

Companion Book By This Author

Leading Edge Trends for AI Driverless Cars

by Dr. Lance B. Eliot, MBA, PhD

Chapter Title

This title is available via Amazon and other book sellers

Companion Book By This Author

The Cutting Edge of AI Autonomous Cars

by Dr. Lance B. Eliot, MBA, PhD

Chapter Title

This title is available via Amazon and other book sellers

Companion Book By This Author

The Next Wave of
AI Self-Driving Cars

by Dr. Lance B. Eliot, MBA, PhD

This title is available via Amazon and other book sellers

Companion Book By This Author

Revolutionary Innovations of
AI Self-Driving Cars

by Dr. Lance B. Eliot, MBA, PhD

Chapter Title

1 Eliot Framework for AI Self-Driving Cars

2 Exascale Supercomputer and AI Self-Driving Cars

3 Superhuman AI and AI Self-Driving Cars

4 Olfactory e-Nose Sensors and AI Self-Driving Cars

5 Perpetual Computing and AI Self-Driving Cars

6 Byzantine Generals Problem and AI Self-Driving Cars

7 Driver Traffic Guardians and AI Self-Driving Cars

8 Anti-Gridlock Laws and AI Self-Driving Cars

9 Arguing Machines and AI Self-Driving Cars

This title is available via Amazon and other book sellers

This title is available via Amazon and other book sellers

Companion Book By This Author

Trailblazing Trends for AI Self-Driving Cars

by Dr. Lance B. Eliot, MBA, PhD

Chapter Title

This title is available via Amazon and other book sellers

Companion Book By This Author

Ingenious Strides for
AI Driverless Cars

by Dr. Lance B. Eliot, MBA, PhD

This title is available via Amazon and other book sellers

<u>Companion Book By This Author</u>

AI Self-Driving Cars
Inventiveness

by Dr. Lance B. Eliot, MBA, PhD

<u>Chapter Title</u>

This title is available via Amazon and other book sellers

Companion Book By This Author

Visionary Secrets of
AI Driverless Cars

by Dr. Lance B. Eliot, MBA, PhD

Chapter Title

1 Eliot Framework for AI Self-Driving Cars

2 Seat Belts and AI Self-Driving Cars

3 Tiny EV's and AI Self-Driving Cars

4 Empathetic Computing and AI Self-Driving Cars

5 Ethics Global Variations and AI Self-Driving Cars

6 Computational Periscopy and AI Self-Driving Car

7 Superior Cognition and AI Self-Driving Cars

8 Amalgamating ODD's and AI Self-Driving Cars

This title is available via Amazon and other book sellers

Spearheading
AI Self-Driving Cars

by Dr. Lance B. Eliot, MBA, PhD

Companion Book By This Author

Spurring
AI Self-Driving Cars

by Dr. Lance B. Eliot, MBA, PhD

Chapter Title

1 Eliot Framework for AI Self-Driving Cars

2 Triune Brain Theory and AI Self-Driving Cars

3 Car Parts Thefts and AI Self-Driving Cars

4 Goto Fail Bug and AI Self-Driving Cars

5 Scrabble Understanding and AI Self-Driving Cars

6 Cognition Disorders and AI Self-Driving Car

7 Noise Pollution Abatement AI Self-Driving Cars

This title is available via Amazon and other book sellers

Avant-Garde
AI Driverless Cars

by Dr. Lance B. Eliot, MBA, PhD

This title is available via Amazon and other book sellers

This title is available via Amazon and other book sellers

Companion Book By This Author

AI Driverless Cars
Chrysalis
by Dr. Lance B. Eliot, MBA, PhD

This title is available via Amazon and other book sellers

Companion Book By This Author

Boosting
AI Autonomous Cars

by Dr. Lance B. Eliot, MBA, PhD

Chapter Title

This title is available via Amazon and other book sellers

AI Self-Driving Cars
Trendsetting

by Dr. Lance B. Eliot, MBA, PhD

This title is available via Amazon and other book sellers

AI Autonomous Cars
Forefront

by Dr. Lance B. Eliot, MBA, PhD

This title is available via Amazon and other book sellers

Companion Book By This Author

AI Autonomous Cars Emergence

by Dr. Lance B. Eliot, MBA, PhD

This title is available via Amazon and other book sellers

ABOUT THE AUTHOR

Dr. Lance B. Eliot, MBA, PhD is the CEO of Techbruim, Inc. and Executive Director of the Cybernetic AI Self-Driving Car Institute, and has over twenty years of industry experience including serving as a corporate officer in a billion dollar firm and was a partner in a major executive services firm. He is also a serial entrepreneur having founded, ran, and sold several high-tech related businesses. He previously hosted the popular radio show *Technotrends* that was also available on American Airlines flights via their in-flight audio program. Author or co-author of a dozen books and over 400 articles, he has made appearances on CNN, and has been a frequent speaker at industry conferences.

A former professor at the University of Southern California (USC), he founded and led an innovative research lab on Artificial Intelligence in Business. Known as the "AI Insider" his writings on AI advances and trends has been widely read and cited. He also previously served on the faculty of the University of California Los Angeles (UCLA), and was a visiting professor at other major universities. He was elected to the International Board of the Society for Information Management (SIM), a prestigious association of over 3,000 high-tech executives worldwide.

He has performed extensive community service, including serving as Senior Science Adviser to the Vice Chair of the Congressional Committee on Science & Technology. He has served on the Board of the OC Science & Engineering Fair (OCSEF), where he is also has been a Grand Sweepstakes judge, and likewise served as a judge for the Intel International SEF (ISEF). He served as the Vice Chair of the Association for Computing Machinery (ACM) Chapter, a prestigious association of computer scientists. Dr. Eliot has been a shark tank judge for the USC Mark Stevens Center for Innovation on start-up pitch competitions, and served as a mentor for several incubators and accelerators in Silicon Valley and Silicon Beach. He served on several Boards and Committees at USC, including having served on the Marshall Alumni Association (MAA) Board in Southern California.

Dr. Eliot holds a PhD from USC, MBA, and Bachelor's in Computer Science, and earned the CDP, CCP, CSP, CDE, and CISA certifications. Born and raised in Southern California, and having traveled and lived internationally, he enjoys scuba diving, surfing, and sailing.

ADDENDUM

AI Autonomous Cars Emergence

*Practical Advances in Artificial Intelligence (AI)
and Machine Learning*

By
Dr. Lance B. Eliot, MBA, PhD

———

For supplemental materials of this book, visit:

www.ai-selfdriving-cars.guru

For special orders of this book, contact:

LBE Press Publishing

Email: LBE.Press.Publishing@gmail.com

www.ingramcontent.com/pod-product-compliance
Lightning Source LLC
Chambersburg PA
CBHW051047050326
40690CB00006B/632